HEGEL'S SOCIAL AND POLITICAL THOUGHT:
AN INTRODUCTION

BERNARD CULLEN

HEGEL'S
SOCIAL AND POLITICAL
THOUGHT:

AN INTRODUCTION

ST. MARTIN'S PRESS · NEW YORK

ISBN 0-312-36674-4

Library of Congress Cataloging in Publication Data

Cullen, Bernard.
  Hegel's social and political thought.

  Includes index.
1. Hegel, Georg Wilhelm Friedrich, 1770–1831—Sociology.
2. Hegel, Georg Wilhelm Friedrich, 1770–1831—Political science.
3. Sociology.
4. Political science. I. Title.
B2949.S6C84 1979   320.5'092'4   79–10730
ISBN 0-312-36674 4

For my Father and Mother

ACKNOWLEDGMENTS

For permission to quote copyright material thanks are due to the University of Chicago Press, publishers of Hegel : *Early Theological Writings,* translated by T. M. Knox, with an introduction by Richard Kroner (1948), and to Oxford University Press, publishers of Hegel : *Philosophy of Right,* translated by T. M. Knox (1942).

Contents

Preface

One of the great problems faced by the reader of Hegel is that he has a most impenetrable style and a notoriously difficult technical vocabulary. He tells us, for example, that the rational modern state which he is endeavouring to portray in the *Philosophy of Right* is the concrete unity of universality and particularity in the Idea. And these technical terms recur on practically every page of his books. My primary aim, therefore, has been expository. Although the Hegel renaissance in recent years has produced some excellent work, there is no concise introductory book on Hegel's social and political thought for the uninitiated reader starting from scratch or for the student of philosophy or politics who has tried to read the *Philosophy of Right* and given up in despair. This book has been written to cater for these readers : I have tried to express the main tenets of Hegel's social and political philosophy in more accessible language, introducing his own esoteric terminology only when I think the reader has been adequately prepared. At the same time, I have striven to retain the richness of Hegel's social and political theory by placing it in its philosophical context.

In the first three chapters, I have endeavoured to answer the question : What prompted Hegel to write the *Philosophy of Right*? An examination of Hegel's early unpublished manuscripts on religion, politics and economics, and his correspondence, shows that his most recurrent theme is the breakdown of community in modern society, occasioned by the development of individual freedom and the institution of private property. It becomes clear that Hegel wrote his whole philosophy as an all-encompassing system, which sets out to render accessible to reason the interconnectedness of the many conflicting aspects of human experience : reason and inclination; the finite and the infinite; self-interest and the public good. The *Philosophy of Right*, then, the mature statement of his social and political thought, is Hegel's attempt to describe the harmonious political system, the rational modern state, in which the conflicts between the individual and the community, between private interests and communal responsibilities, are overcome in a higher synthesis.

The book is not, all the same, merely an elementary exposition : my interpretation does contain some distinctive features. Thus, I have used the concept of harmony—what I call Hegel's 'criterion of rationality'—to determine whether Hegel was, in fact, successful in his endeavour to describe the rational modern state; and I have concluded that he failed to describe the state in which particularity and universality—the individual or the realm of economics and the community or the realm of politics—become harmonised. Nor does the book claim to be comprehensive. Clearly, Hegel said more about social and political questions than I could hope to incorporate into a short introduction. I have had to select those aspects of his writings on politics and society which enable the reader to discern a pattern in his thinking; and I have emphasised those aspects (particularly the sections on civil society and its position in the modern state) which highlight the strengths and deficiencies of his work. In the heel of the hunt, I will have succeeded in my enterprise if I stimulate students to go off and read Hegel's works themselves, with a new understanding of what he was attempting to do; and to examine critically my interpretation. But criticism must be preceded by understanding.

I wish to pay tribute to T. M. Knox for his translations of Hegel's *Early Theological Writings, Political Writings* and *Philosophy of Right*. I have used Knox's translation, where available, changing only a word here and there to capture a particular nuance of Hegel's meaning. All other translations of Hegel are my own.

It was my friend and former teacher Frithjof Bergmann who first suggested that I look at the notion of harmony in my search for Hegel's 'criterion of rationality' (see Bibliography). I am greatly indebted to him, and to John Bennett, Alfred Meyer and Allen Wood, for their encouragement and most helpful comments on earlier drafts of the book. I would like to express my appreciation to Sinéad Smyth for her help in preparing the typescript. Finally, thanks to Jean, not only for living with Hegel for the past five years (in a kind of speculative *ménage à trois*), but also for her invaluable assistance, editorial and secretarial, in the preparation of this book.

B.C.
Belfast
November 1978

ABBREVIATIONS
(for details see Bibliography)

AEM	Schiller, *On the Aesthetic Education of Man*
BH	*Briefe von und an Hegel (Hegel's Correspondence)*
DHE	*Dokumente zu Hegels Entwicklung (Documents on Hegel's Development)*
E	Rousseau, *Émile*
ED	Hegel, *Erste Druckschiften (Early Publications)*
ETW	Hegel, *Early Theological Writings*
HL	Rosenkranz, *Hegels Leben (Hegel's Life)*
HPW	*Hegel's Political Writings*
HTJ	*Hegels Theologische Jugendschriften (Early Theological Writings)*
JR	Hegel, *Jenenser Realphilosophie*
PR	Hegel, *Philosophy of Right*
SC	Rousseau, *The Social Contract and Discourses*
SPR	Hegel, *Schriften zur Politik und Rechtsphilosophie (Writings on Politics and the Philosophy of Right)*

Chronology

1770   Birth of Georg Wilhelm Friedrich Hegel, 27 August, in Stuttgart.

1778   (Death of Rousseau).

1788   Hegel enters the Protestant seminary attached to the University of Tübingen.

1789   (French Revolution).

1793   'Tübingen Fragment on Folk Religion' (published 1907). Graduates from Tübingen, takes up position as private tutor in Bern, Switzerland.

1794   (9 thermidor, Robespierre executed in Paris).

1795   (Schiller's *On the Aesthetic Education of Man*).

1795/6 'The Positivity of the Christian Religion' (published 1907).

1797   'On the Recent Domestic Affairs of Wurtemburg' (fragment published 1913). Hegel takes up position as private tutor in Frankfurt.

1798   'On Love' (published 1907).

1799   'The Spirit of Christianity and its Fate' (published 1907).

1800   'Fragment of a System' (published 1907).

1801   Appointed *Privatdozent* or unsalaried lecturer at the University of Jena. 'The German Constitution' (published 1893). Publishes 'The Difference between the Systems of Philosophy of Fichte and Schelling'.

1802   Publishes 'Faith and Knowledge'; 'On the Scientific Methods of Treating Natural Law.' 'System of Ethical Life' (published 1893).

1803/4 *Realphilosophie I* (lectures published 1932).

1805/6 *Realphilosophie II* (lectures published 1931).

1806   Following Napoleon's victory at the battle of Jena, Hegel forced to flee.

1807   Publication of *Phenomenology of Spirit*.
       Becomes editor of *Bamberger Zeitung* (newspaper).
1808   Hegel becomes headmaster and philosophy teacher at Nuremberg *Gymnasium* (high school).
1812   *Science of Logic*, Vols I and II.
1816   *Science of Logic*, Vol III.
       Becomes Professor of Philosophy at Heidelberg.
1817   *Encyclopaedia of the Philosophical Sciences* (one-volume system).
1818   Accepts Chair of Philosophy at Berlin.
       (Birth of Marx.)
1821   *Philosophy of Right*.
1827   *Encyclopaedia* (revised and greatly enlarged edition).
1829   Elected Rector of the University of Berlin.
1830   *Encyclopaedia* (third revised ed.).
1831   14 November, Hegel dies suddenly.

Hegel's Earliest Writings on Religion, Politics and Economics

The Goethezeit *and Folk Religion*

Hegel's philosophical attempt to surmount the fragmentations and contradictions of his time—both within each individual and between the individual and society—can only be fully appreciated within the context of the living drama which prompted in him the need for philosophy. There is ample evidence that social and political preoccupations—both theoretical and actual—were extremely important to Hegel from the very earliest days: they not only went hand in hand with his religious and metaphysical concerns, but they preceded them. The young Hegel was both passionately moved by political ideals and closely attuned to political reality. In my first three chapters, therefore, I shall sketch the formative influences on Hegel prior to the first formulation of his 'philosophy of objective spirit' in the 'System der Sittlichkeit' (System of Ethical Life) (1802): both the intellectual and cultural influences which contributed to young Hegel's *Gedankenwelt*, and the great world-historical events of the time. Such a survey of Hegel's early development will also greatly help us to understand the problems which Hegel later confronted in the mature statement of his social and political thought, the *Philosophy of Right* (1821), and his suggested solutions to those problems.

Hegel's earliest ideals, while still a schoolboy at the *Gymnasium* in Stuttgart, were largely those of the *Goethezeit*, the prevailing intellectual and artistic climate in Germany in the final quarter of the eighteenth century.[1] Foremost among these ideals was a dual concept of harmony: harmony within each individual; and harmonious relations between individuals in a closely-knit community, in stark contrast to the fragmentation and social divisions of contemporary Germany.

There were two main factors responsible for the emphasis on personal and social harmony among Hegel's generation and the preceding one. In the first place, ancient Greece and particularly Periclean Athens, was commonly regarded as a model of the integrated society for which German intellectuals yearned, in comparison with which German and, indeed, European society was depressingly fragmented and enervated. From their studies of Greek culture, the German exponents of 'Storm and Stress'—the generation immediately preceding Hegel's—had developed an ideal of the harmoniously developed Athenian, whose capacities and powers were fully matured in a cohesive and non-specialised society. (That this idealised picture of Greece may not have been a wholly accurate reflection of historical reality is neither here nor there.)

In stark contrast, the decaying German Reich was at this time hopelessly divided on political and religious grounds. The Thirty Years' War over religion had devastated the country; and in 1789 Germany remained divided into 314 independent and, for the most part, mutually hostile territories. In each of these territories, wherein feudal serfdom remained practically inviolate, the nobility exercised despotic power. To economic, political and religious divisions could be added profound cultural divisions : 'Courts, courtiers and anyone who wielded power at Court took France, its courtly manners and its civilisation as the guiding light. Its general adoption of the French language alone set the political élite apart from the people.'[2] In short, German culture was in tatters.

In an essay dated 7 August 1788 (three weeks before his eighteenth birthday), the schoolboy Hegel refers to the lack of a national culture in Germany : 'The ideas and culture of the social classes are too distinct for a poet in our times to be read and universally understood' (*DHE* 49). Each of the different German states is divided into various classes, he points out, and each class has a specific relationship to the history of the society of which it forms a part. Instead of history, tradition and literature forming a cultural core which would help to weld a society of autonomous individuals into a homogeneous community (as was the case in ancient Greece), culture itself is a divisive force in Germany, since its constituent classes cannot even communicate with one another. Already, before he has turned eighteen, the theme of fragmentation—both personal and social—appears in

Hegel's work. As I hope to demonstrate, his whole life's work will be a response to this problem.

The second reason for the *Goethezeit's* increasing emphasis on the theme of harmony was the growing awareness, from about 1770 on, of the works of the historians and political economists of the Scottish Enlightenment. The writings of Adam Ferguson (1723–1816)[3] and John Millar (1735–1801),[4] in particular, on the development of modern commercial society and the 'division of labour' in history, provided their German readers with tools for the analysis of their contemporary predicament. Not only did Ferguson exercise a profound influence on Herder (1744–1803) and on Schiller (1759–1805) (philosophers of history who, in turn, greatly influenced Hegel); but Rosenkranz (Hegel's first biographer) reports that Hegel actually read the works of Ferguson while still a schoolboy in Stuttgart (*HL* 14). This was probably Hegel's first exposure to political economy; again, it shows his interest in such matters from a very early age.

Ferguson's main concern, in his *Essay on the History of Civil Society,* was to trace the progress of mankind from 'small and rude societies' to 'polished and commercial nations'. Almost in passing, he mentioned some of the less desirable side-effects which the modern 'state of complication' had on the character of modern man, as a result of the concomitant division of labour and increasing specialisation : 'Many mechanical arts, indeed, succeed best under a total suppression of sentiment and reason; and ignorance is the mother of industry as well as of superstition. . . . Manufactures accordingly prosper most where the mind is least consulted, and where the workshop may, without any great effort of imagination, be considered as an engine, the parts of which are men.'[5] Such a description of factory labour was to have a profound influence later, not only on Hegel but on Marx (1818–83).

Ferguson went on, however, to refer to an even more debilitating specialisation : 'Thinking itself, in this age of separations, may become a peculiar craft.'[6] Herder was convinced that—in Germany, at least—this radical separation of human powers had, in fact, already occurred.[7] The problem was not simply that men were isolated from one another because of their various occupations. The human person was thought of as being deeply divided *within* himself, at odds with himself.

This 'divided self' of the human personality was fully articulated

and given a degree of philosophical justification in the influential
works of Kant (1724–1804), who saw man as an inwardly cleft
being. There is a deep split within the human psyche, Kant argued,
between reason and passion, between duty and inclination. It is
precisely this fundamental Kantian dichotomy, between reason
and sense or passion, that Hegel attempted to reconcile in his
Master's dissertation at Tübingen in 1790 : 'Sense and reason
coalesce together in such a way that each faculty might constitute
one subject' (quoted in *HL* 36). This is one of the earliest examples
of Hegel's life-long attempt to reconcile conflicting aspects of the
human person, so that men might live a more truly human life.

A contemporary of Hegel's at Tübingen said of his fellow-
seminarian, in a newspaper interview some years later : 'Metaphysics
was certainly not Hegel's special interest during the four years that
I knew him well [1788–92]. His hero was Rousseau, whose *Émile,
Social Contract* and *Confessions* he read constantly' (*DHE* 430).
Rousseau (1712–78) had been vitally concerned with the growing
atomisation and fragmentation of modern society, in terms very
similar to those of Ferguson. He summed up his view of the situation
thus : 'We have physicists, geometricians, chemists, astronomers,
poets, musicians and painters in plenty; but we have no longer a
citizen among us' (*SC* 22). Indeed, the conflict between the self-
interest of the individual and the duties imposed by the citizen's
membership of a society permeates the work of Hegel's 'hero'. A
fundamental distinction between natural or independent man
('l'homme de la nature') and social man ('l'homme de l'homme')
(*E* 216) is implicit throughout his writings. Man is born free, but in
modern civil society he is enchained at birth, enslaved by his obliga-
tions before the law, to other men and to their institutions; this, for
Rousseau, is the fundamental contradiction underlying modern
political theory and practice (*E* 10).

In his *Émile*, therefore, faced with the problem of how to educate
his fictitious pupil, Rousseau concludes that it is impossible to
reconcile the two contradictory aspects : 'Forced to counteract either
nature or the influence of social institutions, one must choose to
produce either a man [*homme*] or a citizen [*citoyen*] : for it is
impossible to do both' (*E* 7). Rousseau scathingly attacks modern
methods of education which attempt precisely this and end up
failing on both scores : such education 'succeeds only in producing
men of two minds [*hommes doubles*], men who put on a show of

considering the wishes of others but who really think of no one but themselves' (*E* 8–9).

Rousseau's 'natural man' is completely self-sufficient, a complete entity unto himself ('l'entier absolu'). The true *citoyen*, on the other hand, no longer regards himself as an isolated individual, but as an integral part of the community : 'A citizen of Rome was neither Caius nor Lucius; he was a Roman' (*E* 7). He cites the example of the Spartan mother, unmoved by news of the death of her five sons, who rushes to the temple to give thanks to the gods for the Spartan victory (*E* 8). She was a true citizen.

The Social Contract (1762) was Rousseau's attempt to harmonise the two disparate elements of modern man. As he expressed the difficulty himself : 'The problem is to find a form of association which will defend and protect with the whole common force the person and goods of each associate, and in which each, while uniting himself with all, may still obey himself alone, and remain as free as before' (*SC* 174). The solution to the problem lies in a single clause of the contract : 'The total alienation of each associate, together with all his rights, to the whole community' (*SC* 174). We place our whole person 'under the supreme direction of the general will' (*SC* 175). So that we may retain our individuality, the law to which we give our allegiance must be like the laws of nature, implacable and without human discretion. We give up our individual rights to the *community*, not to any specific individuals. In this way, no one leaves himself at the mercy of another. There is no conflict between the individual and the state, claims Rousseau; man is still free, because in obeying the law he is now following his own *generalised* will. While the law is now an instrument to suppress all direct relationships between individuals (thereby ruling out the conflicts highlighted, for example, by Hobbes), the fact remains that Rousseau's social contract demands the total self-alienation of the individual to an impersonal community. It is this which prompted Voltaire's criticism of Rousseau, 'a quite mischievous madman' : 'I found his Social Contract very unsocial'.[8]

If Rousseau did not solve the problem of bourgeois man, however, it is to his considerable credit that he was the first to articulate the antagonism between the private individual and the citizen in bourgeois society. This problem reappears, under various guises, as the realistic core of Hegel's system. Like many of his generation at Tübingen, the young Hegel turned longingly to the ancient Greek city-state, the *polis*, in which harmony had seemed to prevail between the intellectual and artistic endeavours of the citizens and their social and political activities. His ideal was the *zoon politikon*, the whole man who realised his full potentialities within an integrated, cohesive, political community. It is not surprising, therefore, that his writings of this period constitute a hymn to the Greek *polis*, his primary concern being 'to restore man's humanity in its entirety' (*ETW* 212).

Underlying the living unity of all spheres of the Greek national culture was what Hegel called the *Volksgeist* : 'The spirit of a people is its history, its religion, its degree of political freedom— neither the distinct influence of each of these, nor their respective character, can be examined separately; they are interwoven in one bond' (*HTJ* 27). Folk religion was taken by Hegel to be the core of the Greek *Volksgeist*, which encouraged the harmony and totality characteristic of the *polis*. 'Private religion,' on the other hand, 'is concerned with forming the morality of one individual person' (*HTJ* 27). And modern Christianity—especially Protestantism—is 'private religion' *par excellence* : 'Our religion wishes to train people to be citizens of heaven with their gaze ever fixed on high, who will thereby be strangers to human feelings' (*HTJ* 27). Christianity has encouraged the neglect of social and political morality, has stressed private salvation as opposed to civic and communal responsibilities, thereby contributing in large measure to the modern loss of community.

It is quite likely that Hegel inherited his strong views on the socially disruptive nature of Christianity from Rousseau, whom he was reading avidly at this time. Christianity, says Rousseau in *The Social Contract*, was guilty of shattering social unity by offering the individual a life independent of his life in the community. Consequently, he condemns Christianity for making a fundamental distinction between the realm of politics and the realm of theology : 'All that destroys social unity is worthless' (*SC* 272). He is acutely aware that, while all the ancient religions were national, patriotic religions, the kingdom of Jesus Christ is not of this world. Rousseau goes on to recommend that what is needed in contemporary society, as a means of cementing the individual citizens together in a common purpose, is a *religion civile*. This civil religion would have a kind of credo comprised of dogmas indispensable for civil life and imposed on citizens as laws of the state : 'social sentiments without which a man cannot be a good citizen or a faithful subject' (*SC* 276). Anyone who refused to subscribe to these tenets of civil faith would be banished from the state, 'not for impiety, but as an anti-social being' (*SC* 276). Rousseau's ideas on a national or civil religion were closely mirrored in Hegel's reflections on the contrasts between Greek folk religion (*Volksreligion*) and Christianity, written while he was a student at the Tübingen Seminary.[9]

Hegel turned to Greek folk religion as a splendid example of the unity of national life and religious belief. I wish to emphasise that his concern in the writings of this period was not primarily *theological*, in the sense that he was not interested in the truth or falsity of any particular set of religious doctrines.[10] Walter Kaufmann goes so far as to suggest that Hegel's early works should be retitled *Hegel's Antitheological Writings*;[11] and Georg Lukács claims that the attribution of a 'theological' period to Hegel's development is 'a reactionary legend.'[12] But this may be overstating the point, since the works do deal with the social and political effects of different types of *religion*. Hegel's primary concern—as it was throughout his life and work—was the search for harmony and wholeness; and not just harmony in the mind of the philosopher, but real, tangible, creative harmony in the life of each citizen. Harmony which would remove the compartmentalisation and fragmentation which he regarded as characteristic of his age. In these writings of the Tübingen period, he felt that such an effect could only be achieved by the creation of a folk religion in Germany, integrated into the life of the community, which would find its gods, its symbolism and its ritual in the history and traditions of the people and thus provide the core of the common culture, the *Volksgeist*. This popular religion he conceived as kinship with one's antecedents, with one's people and with the natural universe.

A true folk religion should serve the people, expressing and conserving their best values and satisfying their deepest aspirations. This is Hegel's first reference to what he was later to call *Sittlichkeit*, the 'ethical life' of a people. Religion should not be learned from books or reduced to dogma and moral rules to be memorised. Rather it should be a power permeating the whole life of a people : their habits, ideals, customs and festivals, their hearts and wills, their deeds as well as their thoughts and imagination. Religion should be popular, not mediated by priests; there should be no special Church to come between the people and their gods. Unlike the gloomy religion of the cross, it should appeal to the senses and the emotions and not just to the intellect. (Here again, Hegel was challenging the Kantian dichotomy between reason and inclination.) It should not be scholastic but should embody the beauty of the culture, as Greek religion had done.

Religion should not be confined to the sphere of the private person (Hegel calls this *'Privatreligion'*), but should be an integral part of the community. It should not be otherworldly but specifically human : 'The public festivals of the Greeks were all religious festivals. . . . Everything, even the bacchanalian orgies, was sacred to some god' (*HTJ* 26–7). The Greeks loved to honour a god or a hero who had performed some service for the state. Christianity, in contrast, seeks to make men 'citizens of heaven'. With eyes fixed on the sky, the Christian loses sight of all 'human feelings' (*HTJ* 27).

Christianity is guilty of destroying the vital union of the human and the divine : 'At our greatest public festival, one approaches the celebration of the sacred gift in the colour of mourning and with downcast eyes. . . . In contrast, the Greeks approached the altars of their gods, laden with the friendly gifts of nature, festooned with flowers, arrayed in the colours of rejoicing, their open countenances inviting to friendship and love and radiating good cheer' (*HTJ* 27).

Christianity as a Symptom of an Unfree Society

When Hegel moved from Tübingen to Bern in 1793 to become a private tutor, he continued his analyses of religious attitudes and institutions, the main result of his labours being the series of fragments published under the title 'The Positivity of the Christian Religion'. Once again, folk religion—one could almost say paganism in general—is compared to Christianity.

> Every nation has its own imagery, its gods, angels, devils, or saints who live on in the nation's traditions, whose stories and deeds the nurse tells to her charges and so wins them over by impressing their imagination. . . . In addition to these creatures of the imagination, there live in the memory of most nations, especially free nations, the ancient heroes of their country's history. . . . These heroes do not live solely in their nation's imagination; their history, the recollection of their deeds, is

linked with public festivals, national games, with many of the state's domestic institutions or foreign affairs, with well-known houses and districts, with public memorials and temples (*ETW* 145–6).

Religion in these lands served to unify and preserve national traditions : 'Anyone who did not know the history of the city, the culture, and the laws of Athens could almost have learned them from the festivals if he had lived a year within its gates' (*ETW* 147). For at these religious festivals, even 'the Athenian citizen whose poverty deprived him of the chance to vote in the public assembly, or who even had to sell himself as a slave, still knew as well as Pericles or Alcibiades who Agamemnon and Oedipus were when Sophocles or Euripides brought them on the stage as noble types of beautiful and sublime manhood or when Phidias or Apelles exhibited them as pure models of physical beauty' (*ETW* 147–8).

In modern Europe, on the other hand, the national imagery fostered and preserved by a healthy folk religion—an imagery which in turn helps to promote national unity and cohesiveness— has disappeared : 'the imagery of our more educated classes has an entirely different orbit from that of the common people, and the latter do not understand in the least the characters and scenes of those authors and artists who cater for the former' (*ETW* 147). (This is an echo of Hegel's earlier complaint, in his schoolboy essay, about the lack of a shared general culture in Germany (*DHE* 49).) The importance of one other factor is recognised, for its part in strengthening the intimate bonds between the gods and the hearts of men : popular religion singled out certain places where sacred and national history had been enacted, thereby satisfying the need for the living presence of gods and national heroes. In this way, Hegel accounted for the special importance of the autochthonous divinities of Greece (and, indeed, the local and national patron saints of Catholicism) (*ETW* 149–50).

Christianity had not only failed lamentably to become incorporated into the imagination of the peoples who adopted it; on the contrary, it downgraded it to the level of unenlightened superstition. This is precisely what had happened in Germany :

The ancient Germans too, the Gauls, the Scandinavians, had their Valhalla [the home of their gods] as well as their heroes who lived in their songs, whose deeds inspired them in battle or filled their souls with great resolves on festal occasions; and they had their sacred groves where these deities drew nearer to them. Christianity has emptied Valhalla, felled the sacred groves, extirpated the national imagery as a shameful superstition, as a devilish poison, and given us instead the imagery of a nation whose climate, laws, culture, and interests are strange to us and whose history has no connection whatever with our own (*ETW* 146).

Instead of a Charlemagne or a Frederick Barbarossa, modern Germans are offered a David or a Solomon.

These comparisons between the cultural and historical richness of pagan folk religion and the sterile other-worldliness of Christianity now prompted Hegel to try to account for 'the supplanting of paganism by Christianity' (*ETW* 152). How could Christianity, with its socially and personally divisive effects, possibly have destroyed the harmony of folk-religion? 'How strong must the counterweight have been to overcome the power of a psychical habit which was not isolated, as our religion frequently is today, but was intertwined in every direction with all men's capacities and most intimately interwoven even with the most spontaneously active of them?' (*ETW* 153).

Hegel rejects the conventional view that the people were convinced by the sheer weight of evidence that showed their folk religions to be intellectually untenable : as he points out—in reference to the somewhat 'un-Christian' methods of some Christian conquests—'in the expansion of Christianity use was made of anything and everything rather than reason and intellect' (*ETW* 153). In any case, the heathen were not only intelligent, but 'in everything great, beautiful, noble, and free they are so far our superiors that we can hardly make them our examples but rather look up to them as a different species at whose achievements we can only marvel' (*ETW* 153). No, this great turning point in history 'must have been preceded by a still and secret revolution in the spirit of the age' (*ETW* 152). The solution to the puzzle lay in 'the character of the age' which made this bizarre transition possible (*ETW* 154). At this point, political and economic elements emerge explicitly in Hegel's work for the first time.

As in almost all of his writings in this decade, in these manuscripts Greek folk religion stands out in glowing contrast to Judaism, the Christianity of the early Church and modern Christianity. But the emphasis now shifts, slightly but perceptibly, from a primarily religious analysis of the contemporary German malaise to one which took more into account the social and political conditions which underlay the Greek and Christian religious attitudes. In the earlier fragments, Hegel seemed to be saying that contemporary social fragmentation was largely the *result* of a particular form of private, otherworldly religion. And these personal and social divisions could be healed by the reinstitution of a folk religion in modern Germany. Now, however, he concludes that the Christian religion—in both its earlier and later forms—is but a *symptom* of an underlying social, political and (mentioned for the first time) economic malaise: the crucial element in this malaise is seen to be the relation between the individual and a state from which he is 'estranged', in which the citizen no longer has any active political interest.

'Greek and Roman religion was a religion for free peoples only, and, with the loss of freedom, its significance and strength, its fitness to men's needs, were also bound to perish' (*ETW* 154).

Greeks and Romans had been free; and, as free citizens, they were quite happy with their individual, rather anthropomorphic gods: 'Greeks and Romans were satisfied with gods so poorly possessed of human weakness, only because they had the eternal and subsistent within their own hearts' (*ETW* 157). This 'eternal and subsistent' was their intimate relationship with their state, towards which they directed all their energies: 'As free men, the Greeks and Romans obeyed laws laid down by themselves, obeyed men whom they themselves had appointed to office, waged wars on which they had themselves decided, gave their property, exhausted their passions, and sacrificed their lives by thousands for an end which was their own. . . . In public as in private and domestic life, every individual was a free man, one who lived by his own laws' (*ETW* 154). Because he was a free man, there was no distinction made between the public and private spheres of his life: 'Confronted by the idea [of his country or of his state], his own individuality vanished' (*ETW* 154).

Uncontrollable political and economic forces were, however, at work in the world: 'Fortunate campaigns, increase of wealth, and acquaintance with luxury and more and more of life's comforts created in Athens and Rome an aristocracy of wealth and military glory' (*ETW* 155) that eventually destroyed the republic and caused the complete loss of political freedom. Individuals came to dominate the community; the conception of freedom as self-determination within the state was gone. The citizens now felt estranged from the state :

> The picture of the state as a product of his own energies disappeared from the citizen's soul. The care and oversight of the whole rested on one man or a few. Each individual had his own allotted place, a place more or less restricted and different from his neighbour's. . . . Each man's allotted part in the congeries which formed the whole was so inconsiderable in relation to the whole that the individual did not need to realise this relation or to keep it in view. . . . The end they set before themselves in their political life was gain, self-maintenance, and perhaps vanity. All activity and every purpose now had a bearing on something individual; activity was no longer for the sake of a whole or an ideal (*ETW* 156–7).

The citizen had lost all sense of belonging to a people or a state. Self-interest prevailed, with no regard for the common good; the public and the private were split apart : 'All political freedom vanished also; the citizen's right gave him only a right to the security of that property which now filled his entire world' (*ETW* 157).

This change in the social, political and economic realities of their lives had a traumatic effect on the religious attitudes of the Greeks and Romans. The prospect of death now terrified them : 'The republican's whole soul was in the republic; the republic survived him, and there hovered before his mind the thought of its immortality' (*ETW* 157). The citizen died, but the republic, of which he was an integral part, lived on. But now 'the state as the product of his energies' was gone : the republic had died, to be succeeded by an oligarchy that ruled by violent subjugation of its subjects : 'Since all his aims and all his activities were directed on something individual, since he no longer found as their object any universal ideal for which he might live or die, he also found no refuge in his gods' (*ETW* 157). To fill this vacuum, Christianity offered individual immortality : 'In this situation men were offered a religion which either was already adapted to the needs of the age . . . or else was one out of which men could form what their needs demanded and what they could then adhere to' (*ETW* 158).

What men needed most of all was immortality and a sense of belonging. So, the newly-converted Christians fled to the altar, offering up their selves here below and the unhappy present, for the hope of happiness in an eternal beyond : 'They despised the mundane joys and earthly blessings they had to forgo and found ample compensation in heaven' (*ETW* 162). And Hegel—in lines that could well have been written by a Feuerbach, a Marx or a Nietzsche (none of whom knew, of course, of the existence of these manuscripts)—proceeds to characterise Christianity in terms of the most degrading despotism and slavery : 'The despotism of the Roman emperors had chased the human spirit from the earth and spread a misery which compelled men to seek and expect happiness in heaven; robbed of freedom, their spirit, their eternal and absolute element, was forced to take flight to the deity. [The doctrine of] God's objectivity is a counterpart to the corruption and slavery of man, and it is strictly only a revelation, only a manifestation of the spirit of the age' (*ETW* 162–3). (Cf. Marx : 'Religion is the sigh of the oppressed creature, the sentiment of a heartless world, and the soul of soulless conditions. It is the opium of the people.')

By early 1796, therefore, Hegel had forsaken his hopes that religious reform would solve the problem of the lack of community spirit in contemporary Germany. Christianity had not *produced* the fragmentation, the bifurcation between public and private; it was merely a *symptom*, the Christian God was merely a *projection* of the deep bifurcations in Roman and contemporary European life. Religion had indeed helped to reinforce and perpetuate human alienation from the affairs of state : 'The church has taught men to despise civil and political freedom as dung in comparison to heavenly blessings and the enjoyment of eternal life' (*ETW* 138). But since religion was merely a symptom of a deeper social and political malaise, a solution to the crisis could not plausibly be sought in religion. No, the solution was to be found in the liberating power of reason and ideas; and in the translation of those ideas into practice by the establishment of new institutions of state. Hegel asks a significant rhetorical question : 'Apart from some earlier attempts, it has been reserved in the main for our epoch to vindicate at least in theory the human ownership of the treasures formerly squandered on heaven; but what age will have the strength to validate this right in practice and make itself its possessor?' (*ETW* 159). It is clear from Hegel's correspondence of the period that he was convinced that decisive blows for civil and political freedom were actually being struck at that time in revolutionary France.

The French Revolution: Hegel the Radical Political Reformer

There is ample evidence that the ideas and the events of 1789 in Paris received an enthusiastic response among the young intellectuals at Tübingen, the despotic Duke of Wurtemburg having just consented, reluctantly, to some insignificant constitutional limitations on his power. The newspaper reports of the debate in the French National Assembly were closely scrutinised by the students. Hegel, together with Hölderlin the poet (1770–1843) and Schelling the philosopher (1775–1854), his closest friends, was a founder member of a political club which supported the Jacobins and conducted parliamentary debates.[13] Rosenkranz, reporting that Hegel was their most enthusiastic speaker on freedom and equality and a fervent admirer of the ideas behind the French Revolution, recreates the scene, one Sunday morning in the Spring of 1791, when Hegel and Schelling, together with a few other friends, went to a meadow outside Tübingen and planted a freedom tree (*HL* 29) —a gesture which merited for the young enthusiasts an official reprimand. Hegel was convinced that Reason—as it had been conceived by Kant—was in the process of realising itself in the events of the Revolution.[14] As he was to put it a few years later, in a letter to Schelling: 'Let reason and freedom be our watchword' (*BH* I, 18).

This admiration for the ideals of the Revolution—the embodiment of reason in free political institutions—obviously matured during his years in Bern, when he came to realise that religious reform was not enough to secure his ideal of a harmonious whole man in an integrated community. 'Hitherto, religion and politics have played into each other's hands: the former has taught what despotism required, viz. contempt for humanity and its inability to attain goodness, to be something in its own right' (*BH* I, 24). But recently, philosophy had begun to demonstrate the true worth of man: 'There is no better sign of the times we live in than the great respect which mankind now professes for itself : this is evidence that the halo around the heads of the oppressors and the earthly gods is disappearing. The philosophers demonstrate the dignity of man, the peoples will learn to feel it; and, henceforth, their rights will not be trampled in the dust, but they will seize them themselves' (*BH* I, 24).

Obviously, Hegel felt that the people had already seized their rights in France. But Germany's turn was coming : 'From the Kantian system and its ultimate perfection, I anticipate a revolution in Germany. . . . With the dissemination of the ideas [of the philosophers] which show how things *ought* to be, the indolence of those solemn people who always accept things as they are will disappear. The invigorating force of ideas such as those about one's fatherland, its constitution, etc.—however much they may still be restricted—will elevate the spirit; and men will learn to bow down before them' (*BH* I, 24). Hegel was clearly convinced that he was living through a 'revolution in the spirit of the age [*Zeitgeist*]' (*ETW* 152), which would bear fruit in the form of a new constitution in Germany embodying the rights of man : 'The right to legislate for one's self, to be responsible to one's self alone for administering one's own law, is one which no man may renounce, for that would be to cease to be a man altogether' (*ETW* 145). Such a radically democratic constitution would overcome the debilitating bifurcation between private self-interest and real participation in the public affairs of the state.

This version of a community of free men—symbolised by the modern embodiment of the ideals of the *polis*, the French Revolution—is the core of the political thought of the young Hegel. And, as I hope to demonstrate, not just the young Hegel. Age would undoubtedly tone down the youthful exaltation of the Tübingen seminarian. As time went by, he sharply criticised the excesses of Robespierre and the revolutionaries. In a letter to his friend Schelling in January, 1794, he criticised the Jacobin Terror as abstract freedom, the complete antithesis of community (*BH* I, 17). But Hegel celebrated the fall of the Bastille to the end of his life.[15] And the rationalist and secular ideal that he owed to the French Revolution, to the French and English philosophers who prepared the way for it and to the philosophers and writers of German classicism who assimilated its purest and loftiest essence remained one of the constant elements in his thought. He did add to this

B

abiding ideal other ideals which seem to contradict it. The conception of the state which is superior to right because it is the creator of right is in complete contradiction to the conception of the Revolution, which makes right an absolute, superior to all the contingencies of reality, even the very existence of the state itself. But the aims of Hegel's subsequent social and political philosophy were, precisely, to *reconcile*—however much they may appear irreconcilable—the Hellenic conception of the state (the *polis*) and the conception of the state as it was developed by modern theoreticians of freedom and realised by the French Revolution; to safeguard the freedom of the individual *within* the omnipotent state; to show how, in the last and most important analysis, the state is not superior to right or individual freedom, since the state *coincides* with right; and to show how serving the state and dedicating oneself to it is *at one and the same time* dedicating oneself to right and serving individual freedom.

Economics and the Significance of Property

There is one important topic with which Hegel had been concerned from his very earliest writings and which was to play a vital role in his later works : the phenomenon of property. From the very beginning, Hegel demonstrated time and again his interest in the relationship between production and economic affairs, on the one hand, and social and political organisation, on the other. In his Tübingen treatise on folk religion, Hegel had spoken of the ancient Greek as 'fettered to Mother Earth by the brazen bond of necessity' (*HTJ* 28). But the free citizen of the *polis* could liberate himself, could humanise his needs, as it were, through the creative activity of his labour. 'Through his feeling and imagination he so cultivated [Mother Earth], so refined and beautified it, with the aid of the Graces entwined with roses, that he was happy with these fetters, inasmuch as they were his own work, even a part of himself' (*HTJ* 28). This first reference to economic activity is due to Hegel's reading of Locke (Rosenkranz reports that Hegel wrote study notes on Locke while he was at Tübingen).[16] And, sure enough, the Lockean concept of property as the embodiment of the personality of the labourer was to reappear—practically unmodified—in vitally important sections of the *Philosophy of Right,* almost thirty years later (see *PR* §51).

During his stay in Bern, Hegel's interest in economic affairs continued to manifest itself. As we pointed out earlier, the economic and political alienation of the modern world was first seen by him as a consequence of religious alienation because 'our [private] religion wishes to train people to be citizens of heaven with their gaze ever fixed on high' (*HTJ* 27). But he wished to penetrate political and economic affairs more deeply. He made a detailed study of the social effects of the Bernese fiscal system during his time there (*HL* 61). He also undertook a detailed study of the English Poor Laws (*HL* 85). (This is also evidence of Hegel's avid reading of foreign newspapers and periodicals.) Neither of these studies has survived. What has survived, however, is an anonymous translation into German, by Hegel, with notes and a preface, of a pamphlet on the social and political conditions in the Pays de Vaud, which had been under Bernese rule since the sixteenth century.[17] Among Hegel's notes is a discussion of taxation, in which he argues that it is *self*-taxation rather than the *amount* of taxation which is a mark of freedom. In several places, Hegel shows his lively interest in the specifically economic aspects of the Bernese domination of Vaud.

In the religious writings of this period—'The Positivity of the Christian Religion'—Hegel makes many references to economic activity in the modern world. As we pointed out earlier, Hegel came to the conclusion at this time that religious alienation was simply a reflection of an underlying social and political alienation : deprived, during the period of Roman Imperial corruption, of the opportunity to participate freely in the affairs of the state, the individual concentrates henceforth on his own private economic affairs. Hegel makes it clear that this emphasis on self-interest is a regrettable product of a politically unfree society, 'when the purpose of life is whittled down to gaining one's daily bread plus a greater or lesser degree of comfort and luxury, and when interest in the state becomes a wholly self-seeking one' (*ETW* 164); in other words, one is only interested in public life to see how one can manipulate it for one's own selfish ends. Hegel sums up this development as follows : 'All political freedom vanished. . . . the citizen's right gave him only a right to the security of that property which now filled his entire world' (*ETW* 157).

One of the most significant aspects of Hegel's comments on private property at this time is their *tone* : they are invariably tinged with a disdain for riches, a kind of righteous indignation that people should be contaminated by such an ignoble pursuit as the amassing of personal wealth; a pursuit which both was a symptom of and contributed to the profound social and political malaise of his time. There is real bitterness in these lines from a letter to Schelling in January, 1795 :

> Orthodoxy will not be shaken as long as its profession is combined with worldly advantages and interwoven through the whole state. This interest is too considerable for it to be surrendered in the near future; and it is just as effective, even if those concerned are not clearly conscious of it. In the meantime, it will always have on its side the whole vast flock of thoughtless sheep and copycats, devoid of all higher interests (*BH* I, 16).

The tone is even more indignant—with a hint of despair—a few months later : 'At the present time, the spirit of the constitution has entered into an alliance with self-interest, has founded its kingdom on it' (*BH* I, 24). Of course, Hegel had not yet got over his youthful infatuation with the Greek *polis* (indeed, in a sense, he never really got over it). The contemporary orgy of self-interest —and this included the degeneration of the French Revolution, on which he had pinned such hopes—seemed to him to be destroying all possible hope of a return to the social harmony of the *polis*.

It is instructive to contrast this indignant attitude towards the debilitating effects of self-interest and private property with the appraisal of Christ's communism given just a few years later, in Frankfurt :[18]

> About the command which follows [Matthew vi. 19–34] to cast aside care for one's life and to despise riches, as also about Matthew xix. 23 : 'How hard it is for a rich man to enter the Kingdom of Heaven', there is nothing to be said; it is a litany pardonable only in sermons and rhymes, for such a command is without truth for us. The fate of property has become too powerful for us to tolerate reflections on it, to find its abolition thinkable' (*ETW* 221).

Hegel goes on to draw the significance of Jesus's attitude, which he sees as the cause of his rejection by the Jews. In reply to a question from a stranger concerning the division of an inheritance

(Luke xii. 13), Jesus seems to evade the issue by telling the petitioner that to grant his petition is beyond his competence.

> But there is more to the spirit of the reply than that he has no right to make the division, because he turns at once to his disciples with a warning against covetousness and adds a parable of a rich man whom God startled with the words 'Thou fool, this night thy soul shall be required of thee, whose then shall be what thou hast acquired? So is it with him who amasses treasure for himself and is not rich towards God.' So Jesus alleges rights [of property] only to the profane inquirer; from his disciples he demands elevation above the sphere of rights, justice, equity, the friendly services one can perform in this sphere, above the whole sphere of property (*ETW* 222).

The tone now is one of indignation—against Jesus. Who does Jesus think he is that he can withdraw himself and his disciples from the humdrum, everyday world of rights, justice and equity, opt out of the world of property, 'with all the rights as well as all the cares connected with it' (*ETW* 221)? How dare this Jesus attempt to swim against the tide of history, to defy the *Zeitgeist*, the spirit of the age! The tension between the attitudes expressed in the passages above—between condemnation of the debilitating consequences of private property and the confirmation of its historical necessity—is, I think, unmistakable and important. In the next chapter, therefore, I would like to elaborate on Hegel's new attitudes towards property and history at the time of his writing 'The Spirit of Christianity and its Fate'.

The Concept of Historical Development

The 'Fate' of the Modern Era

In his earlier writings, Hegel had contrasted Christianity with folk religion; then he had examined the reasons for Christianity's becoming a 'positive' religion, in the context of its reception by Rome. Now—in 'The Spirit of Christianity and its Fate'—to preface an examination of the reception of Jesus by the Jews he goes right back to the roots of Jewish civilisation. He begins his examination of the spirit of Judaism with a study of Abraham, 'the true progenitor of the Jews . . . ; his spirit is the unity, the soul, regulating the entire fate of his posterity' (*ETW* 182). The young Abraham, born in Chaldea, had been torn away, by his father, from the community into which he was born and brought to live in Mesopotamia. His first action as a young man—impatient for total independence—was to leave his family, for no apparent reason, and begin to wander : 'The first act which made Abraham the progenitor of a nation is the disseverance which maps the bonds of communal life and love. The entirety of the relationships in which he had hitherto lived with men and nature, these beautiful relationships of his youth (Joshua xxiv. 2), he spurned' (*ETW* 185).

Abraham was a man without a people, indeed with no definite ties at all. And he carried this spirit of absolute separation with him throughout his life; as, indeed, has the entire Jewish race. Hegel characterises Judaism as 'the spirit of self-maintenance in strict opposition to everything' (*ETW* 186). Not only was Abraham a stranger to every other person, but also to the earth : for Abraham, the harmonious relationship with the 'Mother Earth' of Hegel's earlier writings is no more. He refused to till the land, but simply let his cattle graze and then moved on : 'The groves which often gave him coolness and shade he soon left again . . . He was a stranger on earth, a stranger to the soil and to men alike' (*ETW*

186). He continually happened upon other tribes who had settled to a life of agriculture, but Abraham insisted on opposing the historical development from nomadism to agriculture : 'he struggled against his fate, the fate which would have proffered him a stationary common life with others' (*ETW* 186).

Hegel claims that this attitude of total enmity to man and nature resulted in the religious, moral and social concepts still adhered to by modern Judaism. Abraham, the isolated individual (indeed, what we would today call paranoiac), felt the need for a deity. Abraham's deity would have to be totally separate also; if not, he could not relate to it at all. 'The whole world Abraham regarded as simply his opposite . . . he looked on it as sustained by the God who was alien to it. Nothing in nature was supposed to have any part in God; everything was simply under God's mastery' (*ETW* 187). There was, therefore, a radical three-way split : Man, Nature, and God. Not only was Abraham foreign to all other peoples; but Abraham's God was just as foreign to all peoples except Abraham's. Worse still, says Hegel : not only was Abraham's God exclusive to Abraham's people, but 'in the jealous God of Abraham and his posterity there lay the horrible claim that He alone was God and that this nation was the only one to have a god' (*ETW* 188).

All in all, a pretty grotesque picture of Judaism, contrasted implicitly with the wholeness of Greek folk religion. Hegel does make one explicit contrast : 'In order to avert from their states [Athens and Sparta, respectively] the danger threatening to freedom from the inequality of wealth, Solon and Lycurgus restricted property rights in numerous ways and set various barriers to the freedom of choice which might have led to unequal wealth' (*ETW* 197). The Mosaic state also enforced property restrictions, but for very different reasons : 'In the Greek republics the source of these laws lay in the fact that, owing to the inequality which would otherwise have arisen, the freedom of the impoverished might have been jeopardised and they might have fallen into political annihilation; among the Jews, in the fact that they had no freedom and no rights, since they held their possessions only on loan [from God] and not as property, since as citizens they were all nothing' (*ETW* 197–8). This contrast is interesting because it shows that the Greek ideal is still strong in Hegel; and also, that he appreciates the harmful polarising effects of inequality of ownership. This latter point will be very important later, in our discussion of civil society in the *Philosophy of Right*.

Hegel's main concern here, however, is a merciless condemnation of the Jewish world outlook: 'The Greeks were to be equal because all were free, self-subsistent; the Jews equal because all were incapable of self-subsistence' (*ETW* 198). To Hegel, all Jews were slaves; they had enslaved themselves to a completely transcendent God. And this could all be traced back to Abraham's initial decision to opt for divisiveness throughout his life : he was estranged from his homeland, from his family home, from his land, from his people, from other peoples; and above all, from an alien God. 'The subsequent circumstances of the Jewish people up to the mean, abject, wretched circumstances in which they still are today, have all of them been simply consequences and elaborations of their original fate . . . an infinite power which they set over against themselves and could never conquer' (*ETW* 199).

Into this situation of personal, social and religious fragmentation came Jesus: 'Jesus did not fight merely against one part of the Jewish fate; to have done so would have implied that he was himself in the toils of another part, and he was not; he set himself against the whole. Thus he was himself raised above it and tried to raise his people above it too' (*ETW* 205). Jesus rose above the many diremptions of Jewish life, in an effort 'to restore man's humanity in its entirety' (*ETW* 212). His goal was integration, on many levels : integration between private and public; between reason and inclination; between reflection and love; between individual and society; and finally, between Man and God, the human and the divine, the finite and the infinite. He came to heal the multifaceted alienation of the Jewish people. But they rejected the god-man. And Hegel suggests that this was the crucial integration missing from Jewish life. 'The holy was always outside them, unseen and unfelt' (*ETW* 193). If God were to come down from his heaven and live and work among men, be seen and felt as spirit in the world, social harmony would follow : 'If the divine is to appear, the invisible spirit must be united with something visible so that the whole may be unified, so that knowing and feeling, harmony and the harmonious may be one, so that there may be a complete synthesis, a perfected harmony. Otherwise there remains in relation to the whole of man's divisible nature . . . the quenchless unsatisfied thirst after God' (*ETW* 291).

The Jews rejected Jesus for two reasons. First of all, they simply did not believe him when he claimed that he was God. Given their whole history and culture, since Abraham, they could not even conceive of an immanent God, a God who was not absolutely apart from Man :

> When Jesus said, 'The father is in me and I in the father; who has seen me has seen the father; who knows the father knows that what I say is true; I and the father are one,' the Jews accused him of blasphemy because though born a man he made himself God. How were *they* to recognise divinity in a man, poor things that they were, possessing only a consciousness of their misery, of the depth of their servitude, of their opposition to the divine, of an impassable gulf between the being of God and the being of men? Spirit alone recognises spirit. They saw in Jesus only the man (*ETW* 265).

This reason for the Jewish rejection of Jesus does not have terribly important implications, since its application was to Jews only. The other reason for his rejection, however, is much more significant in the development of Hegel's ideas. In a nutshell, Jesus's message of selflessness and universal love was too revolutionary : it went counter to the historical development of the Jewish consciousness. So, Jesus had a choice : either he could agree to accept —at least partly—the reality in which he found himself and endeavour to subvert it from within; or he could decide to throw down the gauntlet to Jewish society, issue a direct challenge to its belief system. If he were to follow this second strategy—which, in fact, he did—*he* might be free; but he would be foolishly ignoring the development of history. He would become a 'beautiful soul', divorced from the reality of the people whom he was supposed to be converting : 'With the courage and faith of a divinely inspired man, called a dreamer by clever people, Jesus appeared among the Jews. He appeared possessed of a new spirit entirely his own. He visualised the world as it was to be, and the first attitude he adopted towards it was to call on it to become different; he began therefore with the universal message : "Be ye changed, for the Kingdom of God is nigh" (*ETW* 281). If we cast our minds back just a few years in Hegel's career—to when he was waxing eloquent about 'the invigorating force of ideas . . . which show how things ought to be' (*BH* I, 24)—it is quite apparent that the Jesus of this treatise is almost a parody of the young Hegel himself.

Which brings us right back to Jesus's call for the abolition of private property among his followers; and to Hegel's sardonic comment: 'It is a litany pardonable only in sermons and rhymes, for such a command is without truth for us. The fate of property has become too powerful for us to tolerate reflections on it, to find its abolition thinkable' (*ETW* 221). This is the new concept vital to Hegel's philosophical development: the power of fate. Jesus was rejected because he tried to fight against—or ignore, which amounted to the same thing—the power of fate. Naively, he simply said, 'Be ye changed, for the Kingdom of God is nigh'; and expected (presumably) his listeners to 'be changed'. In fact, all that happened was that 'a small group of pure souls attached themselves to him with the urge to be trained by him' (*ETW* 282).

He sent them out to preach, but they had little or no success. 'The indifference with which his call was received soon turned into hatred. The effect of this hatred on him was an ever-increasing bitterness against his age and his people' (*ETW* 283). He now retreats, disheartened, 'and allows the fate of his nation to stand unassailed' (*ETW* 283). 'The fate of Jesus was that he had to suffer from the fate of his people; either he had to make that fate his own, to bear its necessity and share its joy, to unite his spirit with his people's, but to sacrifice his own beauty, his connection with the divine, or else he had to repel his nation's fate from himself, but submit to a life undeveloped and without pleasure in itself. In neither event would his nature be fulfilled' (*ETW* 285–6). In fact he chose the latter: 'Thus the earthly life of Jesus was separation from the world and flight from it into heaven; restoration, in the ideal world, of the life which was becoming dissipated into the void' (*ETW* 287). Jesus—and Hegel, the enthusiastic young reformer—had been a failure: they had both attempted, unsuccessfully, to impose their own ideas on people and events, against the flow of 'fate'.

Let us now consider the influences which seem to have prompted Hegel to modify his thinking from that of a young radical political and religious reformer to a kind of quietism, when he came to favour reconciliation to the 'fate' of history. I shall discuss these influences under three headings: Schiller's *Aesthetic Letters*; political developments in France; and the political economy of Sir James Steuart (1712–80).

Schiller: the Inevitability of Alienation

In a letter of April 1795, Hegel enthused about Schiller's essay *On the Aesthetic Education of Man, in a Series of Letters,* which he had just read in Schiller's journal, *Die Horen*: 'the treatise on the aesthetic education of man is a masterpiece' (*BH* I, 25). In the fourth Letter of the series, Schiller draws attention to the contemporary discord between man's actual existence in the world ('man existing in time' or 'empirical man') and his true nature ('man as idea' or 'ideal man') (*AEM* 19). Harmony between the two is the goal: 'It is [every individual human being's] life's task to be, through all his changing manifestations, in harmony with the unchanging unity of this ideal' (*AEM* 17). Schiller draws an analogy between the 'ideal man . . . which is to be discerned more or less clearly in every individual' and 'the state, the objective and, as it were, canonical form in which all the diversity of individual subjects strive to unite' (*AEM* 17, 19). This points to a second-level dislocation in the modern world: that between the individual and the state. The danger is that one element in the polarity will win hegemony over the over, 'either by the ideal man suppressing empirical man, and the state annulling individuals; or else by the individual himself becoming the state, and man in time being ennobled to the stature of man as idea' (*AEM* 19).

Both of these dichotomies—between 'existing man' and 'ideal man' and between 'individual' and 'state'—are, furthermore, according to Schiller, reflections of a more fundamental dichotomy still: the dichotomy within the human psyche between 'reason' and 'nature' or 'feeling': 'The law of reason is imprinted upon [Man] by an incorruptible consciousness; the law of nature by an ineradicable feeling' (*AEM* 19). One or other of these two elements must not be allowed to predominate; they must be maintained in a delicate balance. Reason may demand unity, but nature demands multiplicity. Therefore, the rule of rational morality is defective, if secured at the expense of what is natural: 'A political constitution will still be very imperfect if it is able to achieve unity only by suppressing variety' (*AEM* 19).

Schiller has here outlined a series of parallel dichotomies, all of which Hegel was later to summarise under one heading: 'particularity versus universality'. Schiller refers to dichotomies between empirical man and ideal man, between the individual and the state, between subject and object, between reason and nature. When man manages to transcend these dichotomies in a higher harmony, 'man is inwardly at one with himself'; as long as he fails to do so, he is 'at odds with himself' (*AEM* 21). Translated to the political plane, a clash between 'subjective man' and 'objective man' will lead to social disintegration; which, in turn, will necessitate the ruthless suppression of 'such powerfully seditious individualism' (*AEM* 21). A balance must be maintained between 'the variety of nature' and 'moral unity' (*AEM* 23). Schiller suggests that once the fragmentation *within* man is healed, the fragmentation *between* men and the conflict between the individual and the community will likewise be healed :

> Once man is inwardly at one with himself, he will be able to preserve his individuality however much he may universalise his conduct, and the state will be merely the interpreter of his own finest instinct, a clearer formulation of his own sense of what is right . . . Wholeness of character must therefore be present in any people capable, and worthy, of exchanging a state of compulsion [*Staat der Not*][1] for a state of freedom (*AEM* 21, 23).

In stark contrast to the personal and social fragmentation of modern man and his world, in the Sixth Letter Schiller paints a glowing picture of the coherence and totality of life in ancient Greece :

> The Greeks put us to shame not only by a simplicity to which our age is a stranger; they are at the same time our rivals, indeed often our models, in those very excellences with which we are wont to console ourselves for the unnaturalness of our manners. In fullness of form no less than of content, at once philosophical and creative, sensitive and energetic, the Greeks combined the first youth of imagination with the manhood of reason in a glorious manifestation of humanity (*AEM* 31).

Sense and intellect, poetry and speculation still worked in harmony : they all could, 'when need arose, exchange functions, since each in its own fashion paid honour to truth' (*AEM* 31).

Schiller now proceeds to give an account of how humanity developed from the wholeness of 'the individual Greek qualified to be the representative of his age' (*AEM* 33) to the modern victim of 'the all-dividing intellect' (*AEM* 33). He expresses the problem in the form of a paradox : 'Whence this disadvantage among individuals when the species as a whole is at such an advantage?' (*AEM* 33). In the course of dealing with the paradox, Schiller sketches a theory of historical development which was to have a profound effect on Hegel. He argues that the development of the human spirit demanded the disintegration of the 'whole man' :

> It was civilisation [*die Kultur*] itself which inflicted this wound upon modern man. Once the increase of empirical knowledge, and more exact modes of thought, made sharper division between the sciences inevitable, and once the increasingly complex machinery of state necessitated a more rigorous separation of ranks and occupations, then the inner unity of human nature was severed too, and a disastrous conflict set its harmonious powers at variance (*AEM* 33).

The development of civilisation and learning ('*Kunst und Gelehrsamkeit*' (*AEM* 35), therefore, led to specialisation in the sciences and the division of labour. This in turn led to a new form of government, which Schiller characterises as 'an ingenious clockwork, in which, out of the piecing together of innumerable but lifeless parts, a mechanical kind of collective life ensued. . . . State and Church, laws and customs were now torn asunder' (*AEM* 35).

He goes on to paint a picture of factory labour in modern society which one would be forgiven for attributing to Marx :

> Enjoyment was divorced from labour, the means from the end, the effort from the reward. Everlastingly chained to a single little fragment of the whole, man himself develops into nothing but a fragment; everlastingly in his ear the monotonous sound of the wheels that he turns, he never develops the harmony of his being, and instead of putting the stamp of humanity on his own nature, he becomes nothing more than the imprint of his occupation or of his specialised knowledge (*AEM* 35).

The spirit of selfishness and acquisitiveness gains the upper hand : 'the remaining aptitudes of the psyche are neglected in order to give undivided attention to the one which will bring honour and profit' (*AEM* 37). This cult of individuality causes the individual and the community gradually to drift apart, and 'the state remains for ever a stranger [*fremd*] to its citizens' (*AEM* 37). In conjunction with this 'external' split, there occurs a parallel split within the human psyche : 'In its striving after inalienable possessions in the realm of ideas, the spirit of speculation could do no other than become a stranger [*ein Fremdling*] to the world of sense' (*AEM* 37, 39).

Schiller suggests that this twin 'alienation'[2] in modern man was inevitable : 'With this twofold pressure upon it, from within and from without, could humanity well have taken any other course than the one it actually took? . . . I readily concede that, little as individuals might benefit from this fragmentation of their being, there was no other way in which the species as a whole could have progressed' (*AEM* 37, 39). Greek society—as then constituted—had reached the highest possible degree of its attainment. At that relatively primitive level of human development, further development of the human spirit was incompatible with the close-knit, integrated community of rounded individuals that was the Greek *polis*. The ancient Greek could no longer be a 'Jack-of-all-trades', once he wished to become a 'master' in some particular field of intellectual or scientific endeavour.

Schiller now enunciates the doctrine of the historical necessity of the multiple fragmentation of man : 'If the manifold potentialities in man were ever to be developed, there was no other way but to pit them one against the other. This antagonism of faculties and functions is the great instrument of civilisation' (*AEM* 41). The modern world of commerce and industry—with its debilitating divisions of science and labour—is therefore a necessary stage through which mankind must pass. After the simple, unreflective harmony of the Greek *polis*, the fragmented modern world is the second stage :

> One-sidedness in the exercise of his powers must, it is true, inevitably lead the individual into error; but the species as a whole to truth. . . . Even as it is certain that all individuals taken together would never, with the powers of vision granted them by nature alone, have managed to detect a satellite of Jupiter which the telescope reveals to the astronomer, so it is beyond question that human powers of reflection would never have produced an analysis of the infinite or a critique of pure reason, unless, in the individuals called to perform such [e.g.

Kant], reason had separated itself off, disentangled itself, as it were, from all matter, and by the most intense effort of abstraction armed their eyes with a glass for peering into the absolute (*AEM* 41, 43).

The great challenge now, for modern humanity, is to go beyond the fragmentation of modern life and find a new harmony and a new community on a higher level : 'the keying up of individual functions of the mind can indeed produce extraordinary human beings; but only the equal tempering of them all, happy and complete human beings. . . . It must be open to us to restore by means of a higher art the totality of our nature which the arts themselves have destroyed' (*AEM* 43).[3] Schiller was of the opinion that this third stage of harmonious community was unattainable 'as long as the split within man is not healed, and his nature so restored to wholeness that it can itself become the artificer of the state' (*AEM* 45). The only way to heal that split, he claimed, was through a process of aesthetic education, which would gradually overcome the dichotomies within the modern man; this new modern, 'whole man' would recreate a community of purpose appropriate to the higher level of human development.

As we have already seen, Hegel shared Schiller's enthusiasm for an idealised picture of the Greek *polis*. He admired it for its harmony and the absence of debilitating specialisation of faculties and roles. But Hegel—when he came to write 'The Spirit of Christianity and its Fate'—also shared Schiller's conviction that the fragmentation of that unmediated harmony and the concomitant growth of individualism was a necessary stage in the development of the human spirit. And Jesus had been rejected by the Jews because he had refused to acknowledge this, 'the fate of his nation' (*ETW* 283). Finally, Hegel agreed with Schiller that the clock could not be turned back, that the search for a new harmony must take into account the freedom, the self-awareness of the individual modern man. The important difference between the two—as we shall see presently—is that, whereas Schiller felt that the 'wound' of the modern world—personal and social fragmentation—could be healed through a programme of aesthetic education, Hegel sought harmony in a fully-comprehensive system of philosophy, encompassing and harmonising all the modes of experience of modern man.

The French Revolution and the Tyranny of Absolute Freedom

Schiller's emphasis on the development of individual freedom in modern man was the first factor which probably contributed to the dampening of Hegel's enthusiasm for political and religious reform about this time. The second factor was the unfolding of events in France after the Revolution. We can recall how Hegel was convinced that liberty and equality—and, of course, the fraternity of the Greek *polis*—were actually being put into practice in the years following the fall of the Bastille. He had high hopes that the new National Assembly of the Third Estate, having taken over state power from the king, the aristocracy and the hierarchy, would proceed to install a new system of democracy, in which 'freedom to obey self-given laws, to follow self-chosen leaders in peacetime and self-chosen generals in war, to carry out plans in whose formulation one had had one's share' (*ETW* 157) would be embodied.

The declaration of the Rights of Man and of the Citizen had been promulgated in 1789, the 'imprescriptible rights' being the rights to 'Liberty, property and resistance to oppression'.[4] These rights would, in turn, be safeguarded by an administration embodying Rousseau's 'general will' and his admonition that there must be no partial factions in the state and that each citizen must vote according to his own free wishes. At this time, symbolic freedom trees were being planted all over France—and in Tübingen. As Wordsworth recalled when he looked back on the days when he was a companion of the young republicans of Blois:

> Bliss was it in that dawn to be alive,
> But to be young was very Heaven! . . .
> When Reason seemed the most to assert her rights
> When most intent on making of herself
> A prime enchantress to assist the work,
> Which then was going forward in her name.

The army of the fledgling French Republic had beaten the might of Prussia and Austria at Valmy, in September 1792. Heady days, indeed! Then came 'the great metaphysical experiment of 1794, the complete realisation of absolute freedom'.[5]

Between March 1793 and 10 June 1794, 1,251 people were executed in Paris; from 10 June to 27 July there were 1,376 victims of the guillotine.[6] In the name of the general will, the Terror swept away all traces of feudal privilege. 'Liberty must be victorious, no matter what the cost' was Saint-Just's cry. This was the 'despotism of freedom'. Hegel was reading the French newspapers avidly. The Terror prompted him to write to Schelling about 'the infamy of Robespierre and his followers' (*BH* I, 12). The mass of the people and the Third Estate had supported the Terror while it was in the process of removing the fetters of feudalism. This was in accordance with Rousseau's strictures on factions within the body politic. But when the privileges of the bourgeoisie itself—in the shape of its property—became threatened, the Third Estate moved against the Committee of Public Safety, and on 9 thermidor (27 July) 1794 Robespierre—who seven weeks earlier had presided over the Festival of the Supreme Being (Reason)—was himself brought off to the guillotine.

This news from France must have depressed Hegel, at that time in Bern. Feudal alienation had not been replaced by a new cohesive community of free citizens, with harmony between man and citizen, between the private and the public. And Hegel could not possibly even pretend so any longer. Feudal alienation had been replaced by a new alienation, the alienation produced by private interest, which in turn led to anarchy and 'absolute fear'. He pointed out in one of his historical fragments, written during this period, that 'in the states of the modern era, security of property is the axis on which all legislation turns' (*DHE* 268). In the first draft of his pamphlet on 'The German Constitution', written about the same time, he acknowledged that 'bourgeois property' (*bürgerliches Eigentum*) was responsible for the prevailing social and political disintegration. It is likely that Hegel's observation of events in France since the Revolution helped him to arrive at this conclusion.

Steuart's Theory of Historical Development

The net result of this unhappy experience for Hegel was a radical disenchantment with the way in which the Revolution had developed (although he always remained faithful to its ideals). His hopes had been dashed. It had proved impossible to recapture the *fraternité* of the *polis*. He now had to rethink his ideas on the closely-knit, cohesive political community which was his aim. It seemed that too many developments had taken place in history in the period since the heyday of the *polis*, developments of which he would have to take account in a theory of historical development. And his thinking along these lines was aided considerably by his study of Steuart's *Principles of Political Oeconomy*. Between 19 February and 16 May 1799, Hegel wrote a lengthy commentary on a German translation of Sir James Steuart's *Inquiry into the Principles of Political Oeconomy*.[7] (*HL* 86). It has been argued most persuasively, however, that he had first read the Tübingen translation of the *Inquiry* upon his arrival at Frankfurt[8]; that is to say, early in 1797, while he was writing the first sketch of 'The Spirit of Christianity and its Fate'.[9]

Several aspects of Hegel's Frankfurt writings can be traced to the influence of Steuart's *Staatswirtschaft* (the translation of the term 'political economy' in the Tübingen version). First, in contrast to the Tübingen and Bern writings, the focus of Hegel's analysis now shifted from the New Testament to the Old Testament. This analysis of ancient Judaism brings to light a new element in Hegel's study of the historical process: the phenomenon of economic development. Economic activity—i.e. the struggle with Nature—was now seen to be the basis of social and political activity: human self-realisation presupposed the conquering of Nature and the satisfaction of needs. Thus, Hegel's study of the earliest Semitic peoples revealed that their misfortune could be traced back to the traumatic experience of the Flood. This early humiliation at the hands of Nature was the root cause of the subsequent alienation from Nature of the Jewish people: 'If man was to hold out against the outbursts of a nature now hostile, nature had to be mastered' (*ETW* 182–3).

There was also a subtle shift of emphasis from the necessity of political participation to the importance of economic activity. A few years earlier, Hegel had condemned Christianity for fostering political apathy: Christianity 'branded the dominant spirit of the age, i.e. moral impotence and the dishonour of being trampled underfoot, with the name of "passive obedience" and then made it an honour and a supreme virtue' (*ETW* 165). But now, he was more concerned with the fact that Judaism demanded a total cessation of labour on the Sabbath: 'To slaves this rest from work must be welcome, a day of idleness after six days of labour. But for living men, otherwise free, to keep one day in a complete vacuum . . . to make the time dedicated to God an empty time, and to let this vacuity return every so often—this could only occur to the legislator of a people for whom the melancholy, unfelt unity [in a transcendent God] is the supreme reality' (*ETW* 193-4).

Nature itself was seen in a completely different light in the Frankfurt manuscripts. Previously, Nature—symbolised for Hegel in the Tübingen manuscripts as 'Mother Earth'—was the material force from which one derived strength. The free Greek was 'the child of Nature' (*HTJ* 28). But gone now was this sense of reassuring integration with Nature. Nature was seen now as an adversary, to be challenged and forced to submit : 'In need either man is made an object and is oppressed or else he must make nature an object and oppress that' (*ETW* 207). This antagonism between Man and Nature—characteristic of the Jewish people— was by no means inevitable. But it could be traced back to the reaction of Noah and his people to the Flood : 'The impression made on men's hearts by the flood in the time of Noah must have been a deep distraction and it must have caused the most prodigious disbelief in nature. Formerly friendly or tranquil, nature now abandoned the equipoise of her elements, now requited the faith the human race had in her with the most destructive, invincible, irresistible hostility' (*ETW* 182).

Now, there were two possible ways of responding to this show of strength from Nature. The path chosen by the Greeks was one of reconciliation : this was the decision taken, for example, by Deucalion and Pyrrha (*ETW* 184-5). Not so, however, Noah and Nimrod, who held that 'if man was to hold out against the out-bursts of nature now hostile, nature had to be mastered' (*ETW* 182-3). Each in his own way, they decided on a policy of confron-tation, a policy which has persisted down to the present day among Jew and Christian alike : 'Against the hostile power [of nature] Noah saved himself by subjecting both it and himself to something more powerful; Nimrod, by taming it himself. Both made a peace of *necessity* with the foe and thus perpetuated the hostility' (*ETW* 184).

In keeping with this emphasis on relations between Man and Nature, there was a concurrent shift in Hegel's conception of Greek religion. Whereas, in Tübingen and Bern, Greek religion had been praised as a *Volksreligion* or folk religion—the mythology of which was woven into the national history and culture—now Hegel lauded Greek religion more as a *Naturreligion* : Greek religion was now conceived as 'a game with Nature' (*HTJ* 369). There was also a shift in the role of religious alienation. The Tübingen manuscripts, following Rousseau, had held religion at least partly responsible for the political and social fragmentation of the modern world. In the Bern works, religious alienation was merely a symptom of the underlying political and social malaise. When Hegel's historical gaze penetrated further back still, he uncovered *three* stages of alienation in history. Noah's initial decision to wage war on Nature prompted Abraham to cut himself off from both Nature and other peoples. This led to his positing a transcendent God. Religious alienation now consisted of the fact that the Jews had transferred all the riches of Man and Nature into the realm of the deity : 'For they had committed all harmony among men, all love, spirit, and life, to an alien object; they had alienated from themselves all the genii in which men are united; they had put nature in the hands of an alien being' (*ETW* 240). Political bondage and social fragmentation were but consequences of this unbridgeable gulf between Man and God.

Chamley has shown[10] that it is very likely that Steuart's *Staatswirtschaft* exercised an immediate influence on Hegel in the early months of 1797, while he was writing the first draft of 'The Spirit of Christianity and its Fate' (referred to by Schüler as Text 63).[11] Hegel had spent much of his time in Bern analysing the Christianity of the New Testament. Steuart used the world of the Old Testament as a paradigm of a simple pastoral society. From the beginning of Text 63, Hegel's attention shifted to the Old Testament. Furthermore, Steuart was concerned early in his book with the transition from pastoral society to agrarian society;[12] Hegel now wrote about the problem of 'the transition from pastoral society [*Hirtenleben*] to the state' (HTJ 370). So, not only did Steuart suggest to Hegel the theme of economic development in general, but he even seems to have prompted Hegel to examine in detail one particular period in history : the period of the Old Testament. In this earliest manuscript of the Frankfurt period, Hegel analysed the spirit of Judaism from the time of Moses (where Steuart had left off) to the arrival of Jesus. But this seemed to prompt in him the question : what is the origin of the spirit of Judaism? Text 64 (March 1797)[13] attempts an answer to that question. Moreover, the very first paragraph of this manuscript signals Hegel's newfound conviction that the state develops out of the conflict between

Man and Nature. He refers to the Mosaic chronicles and the *Antiquities of the Jews* by Josephus (*ETW* 184); and eventually, the focus of his attention rests on Abraham, the most distant progenitor of the Jewish race.

Steuart had set out, in his *Inquiry*, to trace 'the regular progress of mankind, from great simplicity to complicated refinement'.[14] This 'regular progress' corresponds to the process of economic development from one mode of production, one way of relating to Nature, to another. And the process of development from one economic system to another is supervised by what Steuart calls a 'statesman'.[15] According to Steuart, an enlightened 'statesman' will lead his people from a primitive state of undifferentiated unity (a pre-agrarian, pastoral economy) to a settled, agrarian society; and thence, with the growth of urban life, to the exchange economy of a commercial society. This scenario obviously contains an implicit condemnation of the Jewish race, and of Abraham in particular. And Hegel reflected this typology—and this criticism— in his own study of the Jewish leader.

Whereas the true role of the statesman was to oversee the progressive urbanisation of his people, Abraham had done the exact opposite. He had left a settled life in Chaldea to go to Mesopotamia. Then he had left the highly developed (relatively speaking) Mesopotamia to wander 'over a boundless territory': he had reverted to the pastoral life. Hegel describes Abraham's independence in terms very reminiscent of Steuart. The latter had emphasised the connection between the foot-loose life of the pastoral nomad—with attachment to neither man nor soil—and a certain kind of self-subsistent freedom : 'Where therefore the surface of the earth is not appropriated, there the place producing the food determines the place of residence of every one of the society, and there mankind may live in idleness, and remain free from every constraint.'[16] Hegel says that Abraham was independent and self-subsistent because he 'wandered hither and thither over a boundless territory without bringing parts of it any nearer to him by cultivating and improving them. Had he done so, he would have become attached to them and might have adopted them as parts of *his* world' (*ETW* 186). Steuart had pointed out that Jacob's dealings with other people had been restricted to an occasional purchase of corn; Hegel remarks that Abraham's only acknowledgement of other peoples was his dependence on their corn (*ETW* 186).

According to Steuart, economic development substitutes 'political necessity' for 'physical necessity', which is defined simply as living like an animal. Hegel remarks about the lifestyle of the Jews that 'where there is universal enmity, there is nothing left save physical dependence, an animal existence. . . . Their independence secured to them only food and drink, an indigent existence' (*ETW* 191, 202). Steuart claimed that the main task of the statesman was to assure the steady development of his people through a gradual evolution : there must be no sudden upheaval. Hegel points out that Abraham's fateful decision to challenge the pattern of historical development had exposed the Jewish people to a succession of violent crises : 'These changes, which other nations often traverse only in milleniums, must have been speedy with the Jews. Every condition they were in was too violent to persist for long' (*ETW* 201–2). One could go on citing the many parallel passages which show the extent of Steuart's influence on Hegel at this time. But they can all be reduced to the one important lesson that Hegel learnt from Steuart : one of the keys to understanding the history of a people—indeed, history in general—is its economic development. A study of the evolution of economic forms helps to make history intelligible.

The history of the Jewish people is an example of this. Abraham had gone against the prevailing pattern of world-history : 'He struggled against his fate, the fate which would have proffered him a stationary communal life with others' (*ETW* 186). Jacob also had struggled against his fate, 'i.e., the possession of an abiding dwelling place and attachment to a nation' (*ETW* 189). Jacob finally succumbed. The implication running through Hegel's harsh portrait of Abraham and the Jewish people is that one *ought* to succumb to one's fate, since it involves what Steuart called 'the regular progress' from simple to complicated forms of human organisation. The term 'fate', which Hegel repeats in this context, clearly implies some kind of inevitability. There is a kind of rationality in history. And, just as a settled, agrarian society was part of Abraham's fate, so too is the individualistic commercial society part of our fate; just as it was, to a certain extent, for Jesus. Abraham had struggled against his fate and the entire Jewish people had suffered the terrible consequences. And Jesus had denied the fate of the community in which he had preached communism of property. Jesus was rejected as a result.

These examples of figures out of step with their epoch must have had a powerful effect on the young private tutor—profoundly depressed by the ravages of particularism in his native Germany, the fragmentation of European man and the apparent degeneration of the French Revolution—who yearned for the integration of the Greek *polis*. But he now realised that the harmony of the *polis* could never be recaptured. To think so would be to struggle against the 'fate' of modern Europe. A new harmony was required which would rise above the individualism of modern times, surmount the many forces of individual endeavour in the commercial field and tie them together rather than attempt to abolish them. What was needed was not a revolutionary change in modern society, but a comprehensive philosophical system which would enable modern man to grasp and *understand* the interrelatedness of the many, many forces at work in modern society. To appreciate Hegel's frame of mind at this time, it is not necessary to rely on his correspondence with Schelling and Hölderlin and other documentary evidence : one just has to glance at his descriptions of political conditions in his native Wurtemburg and Germany in general. These writings also serve to remind us that Hegel was continually aware of and passionately interested in contemporary political events; and that, indeed, his eventual search for a system of philosophy was partly prompted by the social and political turmoil that he was living through.

3

From the Chaos of Contemporary Germany to the System of Philosophy

Despotism and Bureaucratic Corruption in Wurtemburg

We have already drawn attention to the fact that Hegel followed with fervent concern the course of events in France following the Revolution in 1789. In 1792, French armies began their repeated invasions of Germany, incursions which brought with them the promise of liberation from the yoke of feudalism. (It is important to bear in mind that serfdom was not abolished in Prussia until 1807, following the victory of Napoleon at the fateful Battle of Jena the previous year.) In short, the turmoil of revolutionary France was spilling over into Germany; and the Province of Wurtemburg was in just such a state of political turmoil when Hegel stopped off at his home in Stuttgart for a few months, on his way to take up his new position as private tutor in Frankfurt. This would have been towards the end of 1796 and the beginning of 1797.

The excitement had been generated initially by a conflict over an aspect of foreign policy between the quasi-despotic Duke of Wurtemburg and the Standing Committee of the Provincial Diet. The Standing Committee—a group of what we would refer to as senior civil servants—was the only body in the province with the power to curb ducal absolutism, thanks to its control of financial affairs; but, in recent years, it had degenerated into an agent of oligarchical power, content with the status quo of corruption and privilege. In an attempt to outmanoeuvre the Standing Committee, the Duke had summoned the Estates of the Province to sit as a general Diet (or parliament), for the first time in over twenty years. The Estates failed to serve the Duke's function, however, so he dismissed them. Among the many pamphlets occasioned by this flurry of political events against a background of revolutionary ideas imported from France, was one by Hegel, entitled 'On the Recent Domestic Affairs of Wurtemburg, especially the Inadequacy of the Municipal Constitution.' It was not published and was eventually lost, except for a brief fragment (*HPW* 243–5). The pamphlet is an excellent example of what has been called Hegel's 'political rationalism' (*HPW* 33). It opens with a rousing clarion call to reform, which appeals to the courage and sense of justice of the people of Wurtemburg. Hegel senses a general feeling of dissatisfaction with their lack of political rights among the people of Wurtemburg : 'Calm satisfaction with the present, hopelessness, patient acquiescence in a fate that is all too great and powerful have changed into hope, expectation, and a resolution for something different' (*HPW* 243). The smashing of the *ancien régime* in France has served as an example to be followed by a people no longer content to be treated with contempt by a despotic Duke and a corrupt oligarchy : 'The picture of better and juster times has become lively in the souls of men, and a longing, a sighing for purer and freer conditions, has moved all hearts and set them at variance with the actuality [of the present]' (*HPW* 243). The longing for justice will not disappear with the passing of time; on the contrary, it will 'penetrate all the more deeply into men's hearts as a result of the delay' (*HPW* 244).

Hegel's early theory that momentous turning-points in history are invariably preceded by a 'still and secret revolution in the spirit of the age'—previously enunciated in connection with 'the supplanting of paganism by Christianity' (*ETW* 152)—is repeated here, in connection with the new age heralded by the French Revolution : 'General and deep is the feeling that the fabric of the state in its present condition is untenable. . . . How blind they are who may hope that institutions, constitutions, laws which no longer correspond to human manners, needs, and opinions, from which the spirit has flown, can subsist any longer; or that forms in which intellect and feeling now take no interest are powerful enough to be any longer the bond of a nation !' (*HPW* 244). Hegel shows considerable rhetorical flair by flattering his readers as to their 'strength of being able to rise above [their] petty interest to justice' as well as their 'honesty to will it and not merely to pretend to will it' (*HPW* 245). He also combines with his appeal a thinly veiled threat of what is likely to happen if they fail to heed his call :

When features and sections of a constitution are no longer

believed in, all attempts to manufacture confidence again by boastful bungling or to whiten the sepulchre with fine words can only cover their ingenious inventors with shame and then pave the way for a much more frightful outburst, in which the need for reform joins hands with revenge, and the mob, ever deceived and oppressed, visits dishonesty with punishment (*HPW* 244).

This is a very important passage, for it reflects Hegel's concern lest the mob-rule which followed the French Revolution should be repeated in Germany, once the 'tottering edifice' of feudal government finally collapses. Read in this light, the fragment is an almost desperate appeal for a gradual and orderly transition from feudalism to modern constitutionalism. Hegel seems to feel very deeply the 'general anxiety that [the state] may collapse and hurt everyone in its fall' (*HPW* 244). The terrible alternative to peaceable transition is a chaotic orgy of petty self-interest resulting from the new-found freedom of 'an unenlightened multitude, accustomed to blind obedience [to the Duke] and subject to the impression of the moment'.[1]

'The German Constitution': the Reich in a Shambles

My purpose in jumping ahead a few years, at this point, and examining briefly 'The German Constitution' (1801), is simply to draw attention to Hegel's familiarity with the social and political reality which surrounded him, while his first system of philosophy was germinating. He himself regarded reading the daily paper as 'a kind of realistic morning prayer' (*DHE* 360). And his treatise shows that he was well versed in German history. The main theme of our study so far has been Hegel's concern about personal and social disintegration—in Judaism, in Imperial Rome and in modern Germany. He begins the pamphlet on 'The German Constitution' thus : 'Germany is a state no longer' (*HPW* 143). The universal power of the state to enforce laws has evaporated : 'Every centre of life has gone its own way and established itself on its own; the whole has fallen apart. The state exists no longer' (*HPW* 146). The self-interest of each 'centre of life' has carried the day : 'Each individual member of the political hierarchy, [i.e.] each princely house, each estate, each city, guild, etc., anything which has rights or duties in relation to the state, has won them for itself, and in this sort of restriction of its power the state has no other function but to acknowledge the loss of power' (*HPW* 148–9). Towards the end of the treatise, Hegel sums up his perception of the decaying German Reich: 'Particularism has prerogative and precedence in Germany' (*HPW* 242). What he means by particularism [*Kleinstaaterei*] is the division of Germany into a multitude of self-governing units, large and small. He deplored this chaos just as deeply and bitterly as his friend Hölderlin, who lamented in *Hyperion*: 'I can think of no people more at odds with themselves than the Germans.'[2]

It is important to remember—in order to avoid anachronistic judgments of Hegel's positions—that Germany at the end of the eighteenth century was not a united nation state such as Britain or France was then, or such as Germany itself was to be after 1871. The old 'Holy Roman Empire of the Germanic Nation' (which finally ended in 1806) had been torn asunder by politico-religious conflicts resulting from the Reformation. In an analysis which foreshadows the emphasis by later writers on the link between Protestantism and the rise of capitalism—most notably by Weber —Hegel suggests that 'the *bourgeois* spirit that was gaining countenance and political importance needed a kind of inner and outer legitimation' (*HPW* 190). The outer legitimation was to be in the form of the growth of small states, independent of the Empire; the inner legitimation was to be Luther's championing of conscience and the free will of the individual as the supreme arbiter in all activities, which in turn justified the political independence: 'The German character betook itself to man's inmost heart, to his religion and conscience, and based dispersal on that foundation, so that separation in externals, i.e. into states, appeared as a mere consequence of this' (*HPW* 190).

Moreover, the rulers of these nascent states and cities—motivated by 'the *bourgeois* sense, which cares only for an individual and not self-subsistent end and has no regard for the whole' (*HPW* 190)— capitalised on this new religious conviction to support their drive for independence: 'The princes could find no better ally than the conscience of their subjects in their endeavour to withdraw from the supremacy of the Empire' (*HPW* 192). In fact, Hegel claims that religion has made 'the greatest contribution to the rupture of political union and to the legalisation of this rupture' (*HPW* 192). The civil wars, especially the Thirty Years War, into which the

Empire was plunged by differences of religion, served to aggravate the drive towards independence; 'and the result of these wars has been a greater and more consolidated separation and dispersal' (*HPW* 190). This situation of particularism was formalised, at the end of the Thirty Years War in 1648, by the Treaty of Westphalia, which 'consolidated generally the principle of what was then called German freedom, namely the dissolution of the Empire into independent states' (*HPW* 198). Furthermore, according to the terms of the Treaty, each of the many states officially adopted the religion of its ruler.

So, this is the situation into which Hegel had been born and with which he was all too familiar. The historian Bryce evokes the absurd situation thus : 'One day's journey in Germany might take a traveller through the territories of a free city, a sovereign abbot, a village belonging to an imperial knight, and the dominions of a landgrave, a Duke, a prince and a king, so small, so numerous and so diverse were the principalities.'[3] In fact, the Holy Roman Empire was a mosaic of some three hundred more-or-less sovereign territories : there were the powerful and mutually hostile monarchies of Prussia and Austria; the several Prince-Electors (of Saxony, Bavaria, etc.); ninety-four princes, both ecclesiastical and secular; one hundred and three barons and forty prelates; and fifty-one free towns. Within each of these territories, the feudal master ruled despotically over his serfs, with a fledgling commercial class cultivating its own particular interests. Relentless repression and strict censorship served to maintain this benighted status quo. There was an Imperial Diet (*Reichstag*), but most of its efforts seem to have been devoted to 'apparently insignificant things like modes of address, protocol in processions and seating, the colour of numerous furnishings, etc.' (*HPW* 150).

Hegel's main concern at this time is that there is no 'common public authority [*Staatsgewalt*]' (*HPW* 147) which would enforce the rule of law throughout the Empire. The Supreme Court (*Reichskammergericht*) at Wetzlar had collapsed, because most of the independent states had refused to accept its jurisdiction over their affairs; and it had degenerated, in any case, into an excuse for corruption and bribery. German law is, consequently, based on pure selfishness : 'German constitutional law is not a science derived from principles but a register of the most varied constitutional rights' (*HPW* 148). Hegel clarifies his meaning in a parallel draft, paraphrasing the old legal axiom that 'possession is nine-tenths of the law' : 'Possession came before the law : it did not arise from the law but was simply acquired first and then made a legal right afterwards' (*HPW* 149).

This absence of a central public authority—in which the independent German states would participate, by sacrificing their particular interests to the interests of the whole—contributed to severe economic stagnation in Germany. Because of the difficulties of building effective transportation networks, and so on, to link up the independent states, Germany was economically very backward in comparison with Britain and France. The commercially powerful Hanseatic towns had been virtually ruined by the terms of the Treaty of Westphalia; Germany had been isolated, commercially, from the rest of the world. Economic and technological development lagged far behind. It was Marx who pointed out, scornfully, that by the time the British textile industry became mechanised, the Germans had just discovered the spinning wheel and the hand-loom.[4]

On the most general level, Hegel substantiates his claim that 'Germany is no longer to be regarded as a unified political whole but only as a mass of independent and essentially sovereign states' (*HPW* 152) by offering a definition of a state : 'A multitude of human beings can only call itself a state if it be united for the common defence of the entirety of its property' (*HPW* 153). There is a suggestion here that the total property of a nation is a kind of embodiment of the national personality which is to be defended as one would defend one's own life. The success or failure of such a defence is not important; the important point is that it must actually be embarked upon. It follows from this that 'if a multitude is to form a state, then it must form a common military and public authority' (*HPW* 154), to raise an army and levy taxes necessary to support that army. Recent history had demonstrated most forcibly that this the German Empire had conspicuously failed to do. And for its failure, the army of the French Republic had inflicted a series of humiliating defeats on this German Empire which existed in name only.

The finances of the Empire were also in a sorry state of disarray. Only half of the taxes levied for defence against the invading French had actually been contributed. Brandenburg had refused to subscribe at all to the upkeep of the Imperial Army. The inevitable result of these fiscal and military deficiencies, according to

Hegel, was the complete inability of the Empire to defend its independence against its foreign enemies (*HPW* 173). And this is precisely what had happened during the recent incursions by France. Hegel heaps scorn on those provinces which called in vain for assistance in their defence; and when their calls went unheeded, complained about the political fragmentation of Germany. Some independent states had sent raw recruits instead of a fighting force; others sent no troops at all; and some sent troops only to withdraw them when danger approached. There had been a general refusal to contribute adequate funds to the war chest. And to crown the ignominy, many of the states concluded peace treaties and neutrality pacts with the French forces, while other territories in Germany were being invaded and pillaged (*HPW* 151). Hegel's conclusion—reinforced by the national disgrace of the defeats by the French—is that 'in its army and its finances Germany does not form any public authority of its own, and therefore it must be regarded not as a state but as a congeries of independent states' (*HPW* 179).

Socially Harmful Effects of Private Property

As we have seen several times before, the spectre of uncontrolled self-interest—in its several guises—haunted Hegel throughout the second half of this final decade of the eighteenth century. He continued to show his concern about the destructive effects of the embodiment of that self-interest: private property. He acknowledged, however, that it was part of the 'fate' of modern man, with which we had to come to terms: 'The fate of property has become too powerful for us to tolerate reflection on it, to find its abolition thinkable' (*ETW* 221). And states of the modern era provided tangible evidence of the power of this 'fate': 'In the states of the modern era, security of property is the axis on which all legislation turns, to which most rights of the citizen refer' (*DHE* 268). Be that as it may, however, Hegel was by no means blind to the cracks in the social edifice caused by extreme inequalities of wealth. In fact, he even went so far as to qualify his criticism of the *sansculottes*, whom he had previously criticised severely for their part in the Terror: 'One has perhaps done an injustice to the system of *Sansculottism* in France by suggesting that its efforts to bring about a more equal distribution of property were due to rapacity alone' (*DHE* 269).

So, while acknowledging the inviolability of property rights, Hegel was very conscious of their debilitating effects, in society at large and between individuals. In 'The Spirit of Christianity', he pointed out that 'wealth at once betrays its opposition to love' (*ETW* 221). We get a clearer idea of what he meant by this if we turn to his fragment on 'Love' (*ETW* 302–8), written late in 1797 or early in 1798. Love is characterised as 'true union. . . . This genuine love excludes all oppositions' (*ETW* 304). Any unrenounced independence, any holding back of a part of himself—from the complete oneness of love—causes antagonism both within the lover and between lovers : 'love is indignant if part of the individual is severed and held back as a private property' (*ETW* 306). However, the union of lovers—the most personal and intimate harmony possible between people—is shattered by the 'acquisition and possession of property and rights' (*ETW* 308). This follows from a conception of property as the externalisation of rights, as an extension of one's individual personality. And this evidence of independence is resented by the lover : 'The one who sees the other in possession of a property must sense in the other the separate individuality which has willed this possession' (*ETW* 308). The property that destroys the unity of their life together is a 'dead object in the power of one of the lovers' (*ETW* 308).

At no time did Hegel call for the abolition of private property : that would be to deny the 'fate' of the modern individual. It is not inconsistent for a philosopher to regard private property as sacred and, at the same time, to criticise the damage done to human relationships and the solidarity of human society by the individual's selfish preoccupation with his property. And this is what Hegel, for the most part, did. In this early fragment on 'Love', then, Hegel was forced to conclude that 'the acquisition and possession of property and rights' inevitably drives a wedge between people, even between lovers : 'Since possession and property make up such an important part of men's life, cares, and thoughts, even lovers cannot refrain from reflection on this aspect of their relations' (*ETW* 308). At this stage, his indictment of the debilitating effects of property was confined to the realm of personal relationships between individuals. However, when he came to write the first draft of his treatise on 'The German Constitution', in 1799,[5] he widened the scope of his analysis to encompass the contemporary social and political fragmentation of which he was painfully aware; and he concluded that the political disintegration of the modern world was directly due to the institution of 'bourgeois property [*bürgerliches Eigentum*]' (*DHE* 286).

Salvation in Religion?

The main concern of this book so far has been to highlight the multiplex fragmentation—both personal and social—with which Hegel was confronted and to which he was most extraordinarily sensitive, from the time he left school in 1789 until he arrived in Jena in 1801. Up until then, Hegel had published only an anonymous translation of a politico-economic pamphlet. He had also written other occasional political and historical studies. He had devoted most of his efforts to studies in the history and sociology of various religions—Greek folk religion, Judaism and early and modern Christianity. His only written work in philosophy had been his Master's dissertation at Tübingen, away back in 1790. I would now like to consider, in some detail, how Hegel came to decide that the solution to the problems with which he was preoccupied was to be found, not in art, not in political reform, not in religion, but in philosophy.

We have already seen how Hegel was deeply sympathetic to the ideals of harmony enjoyed by the pagan citizens of the Greek *polis*. He was to retain this affection for the Hellenic ideals throughout his life; in 1805—long after he had given up all hope of reinstituting such a close-knit community—he called the Greek *polis* a work of art, a perfect example of harmonious totality (*JR* II, 251). But Hegel's readings of Schiller and Steuart had taught him that the Greek *polis* had had its day; it belonged to a bygone phase of human development. The new force in history—individual freedom —had come on the scene to disrupt the pristine harmony of the *polis*. And Hegel was quite savage in his condemnation of those Romantic wishful-thinkers who wrote as if a reversion to such a state of harmony was possible. Social harmony was most desirable; but it now had to take into account the subjective freedom of modern man.

We have also seen how the excesses of the Jacobin Terror in France convinced Hegel that the likelihood of unharnessed freedom resulting from radical political reform was too big a risk to take. So, deeply fragmented as the political reality around him undoubtedly was, he came to the conclusion that it was wrong to *force* the reality to conform to a preconceived blueprint deduced from certain rational principles. Hegel never really had much sympathy for Schiller's conclusion that the ultimate harmony was to be found in aesthetic endeavours. But he did feel up until 1800 that it was possible to 'restore man's humanity in its entirety' (*ETW* 212) through religious activity. In 'The Spirit of Christianity' (completed in 1799), he wrote that 'religious practice is the most holy, the most beautiful, of all things; it is our endeavour to unify the discords necessitated by our development and our attempt to exhibit the unification in the *ideal* as fully *existent,* as no longer opposed to reality' (*ETW* 206). Hegel was thinking primarily, at this point, of the Kantian 'discord' between intellect and feeling, between reason and inclination. He had been attempting since his Master's dissertation, some nine years earlier, to overcome this antagonism between the two aspects of the human psyche. He now felt this to be the function of religion : 'The need to unite subject with object, to unite feeling, and feeling's demand for objects, with the intellect, to unite them in something beautiful, in a god, by means of fancy, is the supreme need of the urge to religion' (*ETW* 289).

Granted the hope of salvation in religion which Hegel expressed in this work, it is important to understand what he meant by religion in these passages. It must be emphasised that religion for Hegel was not the business of going to church and saying prayers, avoiding sin, begging God's mercy and so on, that we usually associate with the term 'religion'. He had already made it clear that the religion of the Gospel was a religion of the individual wrenched out of his social and political environment; it offered purely personal salvation and, as such, was completely unsuited to the task of healing the social disintegration which was such an important aspect of the plight of modern man. And Hegel's god was emphatically not the Christian God. This is important when one considers Hegel's claim that his philosophy is a Theodicy.

Hegel, in fact, defined religion as the harmonisation of those conflicting powers of the human psyche which had been tormenting him for years. Religion, he wrote, is 'reflection and love united, bound together in *thought*' (my emphasis) (*ETW* 253). Understood in these terms, religion, for Hegel, was synonymous with philosophy. And it is, indeed, to philosophy proper that Hegel turned about a

c

year later. By religion Hegel certainly did not mean the Christian religion. The second part of his essay on 'The Spirit of Christianity' was a criticism of the very failure of Jesus—despite the fact that he claimed to be the god/man—to unite the conflicts of man, between religion and politics, heaven and earth, and reason and feeling. Hegel concluded his essay with a final, comprehensive, rejection of the Christian religion—both Catholic and Protestant —as a possible means of harmonising the discord between the different aspects of human nature : 'It is its fate that church and state, worship and life, piety and virtue, spiritual and worldly action, can never dissolve into one' (*ETW* 301).

About a year later, in the 'Fragment of a System' (dated 14 September 1800), Hegel was still using the term 'religion' to refer to the grand synthesis he was looking for. He now gathered the many sets of conflicts afflicting modern man under the general heading of the dissonance between the finite and the infinite; and he wrote that the 'self-elevation of man . . . from finite life to infinite life, is religion' (*ETW* 311). The person thus self-elevated 'puts himself . . . outside his restricted self' and intimately unites himself with the infinite living being that runs through all living beings (*ETW* 312). This infinite living being must emphatically be immanent in the world; Hegel thus ruled out what he took to be the ultimately transcendent Christian God, 'an alien spirit, felt as alien' (*ETW* 294).

In this fragment, Hegel criticised philosophy, which 'has to stop short of religion because it is a process of thinking and, as such a process, implies an opposition with nonthinking [processes] as well as the opposition between the thinking mind and the object of thought' (*ETW* 314). It is clear, however, that Hegel was here thinking of a one-sided 'philosophy of the understanding' (such as the philosophy of Kant) which is concerned with things as separate, finite objects and fails to grasp their interconnectedness. But already, in this fragment, he introduced the concept which could be regarded as the key to his later system of philosophy : that of spirit (*Geist*), 'the living unity of the manifold' (*ETW* 311). And he also introduced the seminal notion of the synthesis in the individual of particularity and universality : 'A human being is an individual life insofar as he is to be distinguished from all the elements and from the infinity of individual beings outside himself. But he is only an individual life insofar as he is at one with all

the elements, with the infinity of lives outside himself' (*ETW* 310).
So he was clearly using the term 'religion' to denote the activity
which he was soon to call 'speculative philosophy'. Indeed, some
six weeks later, in a momentous letter to Schelling dated 2 November
1800, he announced his intention henceforth to devote himself to
philosophy: 'In my intellectual development which began with
the more subordinate needs of man, I have been compelled to
proceed towards philosophy, and at the same time the ideal of my
youth [i.e. the harmonising of all bifurcations] had to be transformed into the form of reflection, into a system' (*BH* I, 59).

Hegel had come to feel more and more acutely man's inability
to feel at one with himself and his world; the ideal of his youth
seemed unattainable. Since the world could not be changed, man's
perception of it must be changed. What was needed, then, was
a radical reinterpretation of human experience, which would enable
modern men to grasp the interconnectedness of the many diverse
aspects of their lives. In his letter, Hegel added that he was cur-
rently working on the formulation of his philosophical system. The
first fruits of his endeavours were published shortly after his arrival
in Jena in early 1801, in an article entitled 'The Difference between
the Systems of Philosophy of Fichte and Schelling'. And, in the
course of an introductory section headed 'The Need for Philosophy',
Hegel heralded the close of the formative period of his career with
the statement that 'Bifurcation [*Entzweiung*] is the source of the
need for philosophy' (*ED* 12).

The System of Philosophy: First Draft

The fascination of this—Hegel's first philosophical publication—
lies not so much in his evaluation of Fichte and Schelling, but in
the fact that he presents here (with greater clarity than he later
achieved) some of the cornerstones of his mature system of
philosophy. Foremost among these is the synthesising power of
reason (*Vernunft*). Reason restores the overall harmony which had
prevailed in the Greek *polis*, when self-interest and the interest of
the community coincided. With the shattering of that original
harmony, man's life became torn apart by conflicts which could
no longer be integrated into the unity of the social totality. And
Hegel sees the history of philosophy as the history of the fundamental conflicts between 'mind and matter, soul and body, belief

and understanding, freedom and necessity'; more recently, between 'reason and sense', 'intelligence and nature' and, in the most general form of these conflicts, between 'absolute subjectivity and absolute objectivity' : 'To overcome such fixed oppositions is the sole interest of reason' (*ED* 13).

Philosophy comes on the scene in a torn world, as the pressing need to overcome the opposition between fixed subjectivity and fixed objectivity 'and to conceive the coming into being of the intellectual and real world as a process' (*ED* 14). Hegel does not wish to claim that reason and philosophy are opposed to conflict as such. His study of history (and the lessons he has learnt from Schiller and Steuart) has shown him that separation and opposition are necessary aspects or stages (what Schiller had called [*AEM* 171] and what Hegel would later call 'moments') of human development : 'Reason attains the absolute only by emerging from this manifold diversity. . . . But reason is against the absolute fixation of bifurcation by the understanding' [*Verstand*] (*ED* 13/4). This, incidentally, is an interesting example of a theme in Hegel's thought which had been germinating for some time. Some three years earlier, in the fragment on 'Love', he had expressed it as the 'process' of 'unity, separated opposites, reunion' (*ETW* 308). And this theme was to be of vital importance for Hegel's whole system.

Separation and conflict are important 'moments' of human reality, provided people do not lose sight of the overall unity of life : 'The need for philosophy emerges when the power of reconciliation disappears from the life of men and opposites have lost their living relation and reciprocity and achieve independence' (*ED* 14). Hegel claims later in the article that this is precisely what has happened in Fichte's *Sittenlehre* (1797). Fichte's account of ethics has given rise to a dualistic conception of man himself : 'When in ethics the governing power is located in the person himself, and a governing faculty and an obeying faculty are absolutely opposed within him, then the inner harmony is destroyed; discord and absolute bifurcation constitute the nature of the person' (*ED* 70).

Hegel goes on to emphasise the crucial distinction between the understanding (*Verstand*) and reason (*Vernunft*). This is the distinction between scientific thought and speculative thought. 'As soon as truths of common human understanding are taken by themselves and isolated . . . they appear distorted and as half-truths' (*ED* 21). We can also think of this as the difference between analytical thinking which breaks reality down into isolated objects of thought and dialectical thinking which perceives the relations between all aspects of reality. The understanding is only capable of drawing distinctions and grasping external relations between determinate atoms or monads, each of which is governed by the principle of identity and opposition : each thing is identical with itself and opposed to everything else. When things change, according to 'the understanding', one thing has ceased to exist (e.g. a boy) and its place has been taken by something entirely different and new (in this case, a man). In this way, the world becomes divided into a multitude of antinomies. Hegel explicitly links the develcpment of this way of thinking with certain developments in the way people relate to each other and to the world. Antagonistic thought-patterns are a reflection of antagonism in the real world of people's lives.

In contrast to this limitation of thought by the principle of identity and opposition, reason (*Vernunft*) can grasp the fundamental unity, the becoming, underlying all things : reason alone is able to 'unite that which was separated and reduce absolute bifurcation to a relative bifurcation which is contingent upon fundamental identity' (*ED* 14). This restoration of totality by reason would embrace—among other instances of harmonisation—the harmonisation of social relations in the community. But just because reason seeks to integrate *all* conflicts in the totality of human experience, Hegel is adamant that philosophy must be presented in a system (*ED* 34).

Another important Hegelian concept which assumes prominence in this article is the concept of spirit (*Geist*). But this is not the first time we have encountered Hegel's use of the term; and his previous use of it in the 'Fragment of a System' yields connotations of the term which are not as evident in the Jena article and subsequent works. In 'The Difference . . . ,' he claims that reality is intelligible to him because it is structured by spirit. The spirit which permeates all of reality is what makes the world rational. And, of course, this spirit is accessible to human reason; if it were not, something akin to Kant's world of unknowable things-in-themselves would be revived to destroy the very harmony which spirit is supposed to recapture.

There has always been something of a controversy about whether to translate the term *Geist* by 'mind' or 'spirit' (the word can mean both these things in German). One of the significances of the term is, of course, that it is meant to denote a synthesis of *both* (human) mind *and* (superhuman) spirit. It is also meant to synthesise the realms of the finite and the infinite—the term *Geist* is used in such phrases as *'der heilige Geist'* ('the Holy Ghost'). The latter connotation—which is perhaps the most important—is brought out more clearly in the 'Fragment of a System'. There, identification of *Geist* with God is suggested when Hegel says that 'we may call infinite life a spirit in contrast with the abstract multiplicity, for spirit is the living unity of the manifold. . . . The spirit is an animating law in union with the manifold which is then itself animated. When man takes this animated manifold as a multi-plicity of many individuals, yet as connected with the animating spirit, then these single lives become organs, and the infinite whole becomes an infinite totality of life' (*ETW* 311–12).

Spirit it is that gives life to the manifold of the world, comprising both Nature and Man. But this spirit, which permeates all of reality, is emphatically immanent in reality; unlike the transcen-dent Christian God, detached from the rest of the world. Man and God, says Hegel, the finite and the infinite, are united in spirit. Because of the way in which it is present in all of human experi-ence, spirit renders God human and Man divine. The bifurcation between heaven and earth is finally united in spirit. Hegel returns to this theme again in a slightly later article on 'Faith and Know-ledge'. He attacks those philosophers, such as Kant and Jacobi, who have placed God in an extrarational limbo. The mere under-standing, of which they are prime exponents, is so tied down to the realm of the finite that they deny all possibility of rationally contemplating God. For such philosophers, says Hegel, 'God is dead' (*ED* 345). But spirit is not dead; spirit lives in and through all reality and it is the task of reason and speculative philosophy to perceive the infinite (i.e. spirit) in the finite, the eternal in the herebelow : 'the highest totality [spirit or God] . . . can and must rise again' (*ED* 346).

From Folk Religion to the System of Philosophy: a Recapitulation

My book so far has been a detailed attempt to answer the question : why did Hegel—at the age of thirty—decide to write a system of philosophy? Why would anyone write those long volumes of the *Logic* and the *Encyclopaedia*? Why did Hegel deem philosophy to be necessary? Through a close study of his works and correspondence when he was roughly between the ages of twenty and thirty, I have tried to demonstrate what Hegel took his task as a philosopher to be. I have shown that his writings of this period consist almost exclusively of diagnoses of personal and social fragmentation : what Hegel would later call 'alienation' (*Entfremdung*). I have been at pains to show that Hegel was acutely aware of this alienation under several different guises : the gulf that had appeared between Man and a transcendent God; also, between Man and Nature; the conflicts between different aspects of the human psyche; and the antagonisms between private and public interests, between the individual and the community in which he lived.

In the course of this formative decade of his life, Hegel considered and rejected several possible solutions to these related problems. In his writings of the Bern period, religious reform was rejected as an untenable solution, since religious alienation was seen to be merely a symptom of an underlying political malaise— the lack of freedom (see pp. 8–14 above). Radical political reform, which would sweep away outmoded political institutions and institute freedom in society, was also rejected as a solution, since the disastrous results of the Terror convinced Hegel that such a course of action would be likely to cause the pendulum to swing to the opposite extreme of unharnessed freedom (see pp. 30–31 above). Hegel finally came to the conclusion that *all* these antagonistic elements of *human experience*—reason, inclination; intellect, feeling; the human, the divine; the natural, the supernatural; the finite, the infinite; egoism, altruism; self-interest, the common good; individualism, collectivism; and the many others—must be united in a higher synthesis. And this was the task of a system of philosophy, which would describe the development of human self-consciousness and would demonstrate the positive contributions of various diremptive aspects of experience; aspects which, considered in isolation, appear to the understanding to be completely negative and destructive of harmony and totality. The unifying element of all human experience and of this system of philosophy would be Spirit and Reason.

Hegel's philosophy, then, is the product of his personal, agonising confrontation with the alien world in which he lived. This confrontation with reality took on many forms, as we have seen. But Hegel's attempt to surmount the bifurcations and contradictions of his time in a system of philosophy can only be fully appreciated if we keep before our minds his passionate and abiding interest in social and political affairs, that living drama which prompted in him the need for philosophy. While it is my contention that *all* of Hegel's philosophy—even the most abstract aspects—is motivated by a desire for harmony in human experience and is thus socio-political, at least implicitly, in the remainder of this book I shall focus my attention on the *explicitly* social and political aspects of that philosophy.

Hegel experienced to the full the many anxieties and the many hopes common to the young people of his generation. He was deeply troubled by the sorry state of Germany : backward, feudalistic and apparently intent on tearing itself apart. His political ideals were community and universality, legacies of the Greek *polis* and the German Enlightenment. It was the very lack of solidarity in modern individualistic, commercial society that prompted Hegel's quest for harmony between the individual and the community. True universality meant for Hegel, in social and political terms, a community in which the freedom of its constituent individuals would be preserved and enhanced.

His hopes were carried by the French Republic, declared in 1789, when Hegel was nineteen. In France, the new Republic was incarnating and, he hoped, spreading to Germany and beyond, the new ideas of the free modern state. A genuinely human world— the work of reason—was being created, he thought, in France; but this merely served to emphasise the utter inhumanity of the reality in which he found himself. The stark contrast between the renewal going on in France and the fragmentation of feudal Germany, divided against itself, was particularly disturbing. Gradually, however, as the atrocities of the Terror mounted up, Hegel realised that individualism was just as strong in revolutionary France as it was in Germany.

So, he found himself confronted with the bitter antagonism between his own philosophical and political ideals and the anarchic social reality which surrounded him. In the modern, acquisitive society, the free individual—alienated from the institutions of state —was turning his attention and ingenuity to the amassing of personal wealth. In the process, great leaps forward were being accomplished in the mastery of Nature by human reason, by dint of developments in technology and the destruction of obsolete, feudal power relations which had hampered the advance of mankind. Hegel acknowledged that these developments—and the resulting antagonisms—had to be pushed to a certain limit beyond which they would be totally irrational and destructive, before the desired reconciliation between the particular and the universal (the individual and the community) could be achieved. In other words, the free play of individual, entrepreneurial forces was necessary, to lay the foundations for the victory of mankind in its struggle to win freedom from the tyranny of Nature. These were the forces of laissez-faire capitalism, which had been developing for some time in Britain and which had now gained political power in France.

In this inhuman, hostile, alien world of unbridled competition between free individuals, the most vital and urgent task before Hegel was to establish a new harmony between Man and the world in which he finds himself, because the highest potentialities of the individual could be realised *only* within a rational community of free individuals, i.e. the sphere of the universal and not of the particular. The individual could attain true fulfilment only if he was a free member of a real community. Gradually, Hegel forsook the revolutionary path to community, which would have meant modelling a new world, in accordance with a preconceived plan, by means of conflict and violence.

He chose another road to harmony—the harmony of philosophical reconciliation—which would not entail a denial of the new world then being born. In the *Philosophy of Right*, he emphasised the therapeutic purpose of his philosophy: 'I am at home in the world when I know it, still more so when I have understood it' (*PR* 4A). Hegel set out to be the theoretical consciousness of the new bourgeois order being brought about in France and throughout Europe by Napoleon, the successor of the French revolutionaries. Liberation came to mean for him self-recognition in reality, the total possession of the new bourgeois world by reason.

4

The Jena Social and Political Writings

The 'System of Ethical Life': Objective Spirit

Philosophy, then, for Hegel, will provide an all-encompassing account of the modern world and its development. In the remainder of this book, we shall be concerned only with the specifically social and political aspects of the modern world; with Hegel's account of the confrontation of the human spirit with its environment and the development of self-consciousness through political and economic institutions and practice. Social and political experience, as Hegel understands it, is not an incidental epiphenomenon of human life (e.g. something we only think of around election time— a duty, perhaps, but a nuisance). It is the way in which Man relates to his world; and, in so doing, develops the powers of his mind. If Hegel's philosophical theory of politics and society is deficient, therefore, such a deficiency constitutes a very serious crack in his entire philosophical edifice. Hegel's first attempt to give a systematic account of this 'philosophy of mind' or 'philosophy of objective spirit' is contained in his 'System of Ethical Life' ('System der Sittlichkeit'), which he wrote in 1802, the second year of his tenure as an instructor in philosophy at the University of Jena.

Since the term *Sittlichkeit* is crucial for an understanding of Hegel's moral and political philosophy, it would do no harm to spend some time elucidating what he meant by it. Above all, Hegel wishes to distinguish clearly between *Moralität* and his own *Sittlichkeit* (these terms are usually translated as 'morality' and 'social ethics' or 'ethical life' respectively). Perhaps the most lucid account of this distinction is given by Hegel himself (quite surprising, when one considers the abstruse passages in the relevant sections of the *Philosophy of Right*), in his article 'On the Scientific Methods of Treating Natural Law' (1802).

The chief object of Hegel's polemic is Kant's categorical impera-

tive that ' a maxim of one's will must at the same time be valid
as the principle of a universal law'. He goes to great pains to
criticise the lack of content of the categorical imperative : 'there
is absolutely nothing that could not be made a law of ethics in this
way' (*SPR* 354). He proposes to substitute for the emptiness of
Kant's *Moralität* the content of *Sittlichkeit* : 'It is in the nature of
absolute *Sittlichkeit* to consist of something universal, of customs
[*Sitten*]' (*SPR* 392). He goes on to formulate the distinction thus :
'The recent systems of *Sittlichkeit* [viz. those of Kant and Fichte],
since they make being-for-oneself and the particular individual
their principle . . . cannot misapply these words to designate their
concern; they adopt instead the word *Moralität*' (*SPR* 392–3).

The point is that, although Kant and Fichte refer to customs or
mores (*Sitten*) in the titles of their works (Kant's *Metaphysik der
Sitten* and Fichte's *System der Sittenlehre*), Hegel accuses them
of misusing the term *Sitten*, since their actual theories have little
or nothing to do with customs or with an ethics based on custom.
So, in order to emphasise the difference between his own theory
and Kant's, Hegel uses the term *Moralität* to designate Kant's
moral theory, distinguishing it clearly from his own *Sittlichkeit*.
The Greek derivation of Hegel's concept is suggested by his fre-
quent quotations from Plato and Aristotle and his other references
to 'antiquity' : 'Concerning *Sittlichkeit*, the word of the wisest man
of antiquity is the only truth : being ethical [*sittlich*] means living
in accordance with the customs [*Sitten*] of one's country' (*SPR* 396).[1]

That the Hellenic ideal of a close-knit and harmonious community is still very important for Hegel is clear when he remarks
that 'the absolute ethical [*sittliche*] totality is nothing other than
a people [*Volk*]' (*SPR* 371). The ideal of an intimate relationship
between ethical concerns and the life of the community, which
dates back to his studies of Greek *Volksreligion*, remains crucial
for Hegel throughout his work.

Because the 'System der Sittlichkeit' is Hegel's first attempt to
work out a philosophical description of ethical and political experience and because he subsequently made few changes in this overall
schema, I shall give a brief account of the relevant aspects of it.
Since my purpose in summarising the 'System' is simply to give
the reader a quick impression of how Hegel's theories are beginning
to take shape at this time, I shall not attempt to go into the details
of his argument or to figure out exactly what he means by all of

the technical terms he introduces. We shall find later, however, that the *Philosophy of Right*—with many modifications in the details—is still substantially the same as the earlier essay. The 'System der Sittlichkeit' (1802) is, in effect, the first draft of the *Philosophy of Right*, published some nineteen years later.

The 'System der Sittlichkeit' is a record of the relations between Man and his world in history; i.e. of the different ways of perceiving the world and of conquering it, so as to satisfy Man's developing needs. Hegel begins by postulating absolute *Sittlichkeit* as the supreme form of ethical life. Hegel does not exactly define 'absolute *Sittlichkeit*'; but it is clear from the context that absolute *Sittlichkeit* is the sum total of all ethical forms, all juridical determinations, all political institutions and categories, etc.; all these phenomena are merely manifestations or 'moments' of the absolute *Sittlichkeit*. The bearer of the absolute *Sittlichkeit* is the people [*Volk*] : the ethical ideal for individuals consists of living entirely in and for the people to which they belong (*SPR* 419).

At the very beginning, Man, the natural world and the community were bound together in immediate harmony. This is the level of what Hegel calls 'natural ethical life [*natürliche Sittlichkeit*]' (*SPR* 421). To satisfy their unthinking needs and desires, men simply 'annihilated' the fruits of the natural world around them. At this primitive level of social and political experience, men had not yet succeeded in distinguishing their own individuality from the unreflective solidarity of the community.

With the increasing complexity and sophistication of needs, men began to labour. This led to the creation of tools, to the acquisition of goods, to the definition of certain types of human relationships (e.g. between parents and children), to culture and language. In this process, natural feeling became intelligence; thought in terms of the particular only gave way to the use of generalities; the things of nature were no longer simply annihilated, but were worked upon and fashioned by conscious wills. Tools were developed into machines, by means of which an abundance of goods was produced; from this the community benefited and private property was created. Such purposive activity presupposes the development of intelligence in Man.

This human intelligence grasped the necessity of an association of conscious individuals, operating a form of division of labour for satisfying the community's needs and replenishing what was consumed. The simple, unmediated unity of 'natural harmony' was broken up and replaced by a spirit of conscious association among labourers. Typical of this cooperation was the development and operation of tools demanding more than one operator.

Freed from the shackles of immediate need, men developed economic relations; and, with them, concepts to govern property relations such as value, price, exchange and contract. At this stage, commerce emerged—having been made possible by the creation of money—and this brought about relationships of domination and subordination. Relations between men, however, gradually became more integrated. Antagonisms were gradually overcome : first in the family; then in the social institutions of labour, property and law; and finally in the highest form of social and political organisation, the state.

The person is defined by Hegel as a free being. But free persons come up against unequal forces and some of them show themselves to be superior to others. Theoreticians insist on postulating absolute equality and rights; but these are only illusory abstractions, claims Hegel. In every group of individuals, there are some who are richly endowed with what is physically necessary for life and others who are deficient in this respect; and this necessary inequality gives rise to the fundamental opposition between domination and servitude. Reconciliation between masters and slaves eventually takes place in the family, within which there is an identity of needs and in which goods are held in common ownership. The foundations of the family are marriage and the child, which represent continuity and stability in an essentially contingent institution.

Opposed to and evolving out of this family organisation, within which the freedom of the constituent members is limited reciprocally, is limitless and unchecked individual freedom. This freedom leads to various degrees of crime : from the devastation of entire continents such as was perpetrated by Genghis Khan, Tamerlane and the Norse pirates, through murder and armed robbery, to simple theft.

Hegel's description of the development of human relations in history also has an important ontological dimension. Corresponding to the historical stages of development there is an ontological progression from lower to higher forms of being. The highest form of social organisation—a people—is the only form which embodies the universal element of human life, spirit. The forms of life which we have just examined—the family and the epoch of absolute freedom—have not yet attained the level of absolute ethical life.

Absolute ethical life manifests itself in a people (*Volk*), the universal ethical category which has a reality for each individual consciousness in the community, which is identical with all the individuals and which wields sovereign power over them. As members of a people, isolated individuals form an identity and recognise themselves in their compatriots, since those compatriots also participate in the spirit which runs through the whole people. A people is 'not an unrelated multitude' of individuals, but an 'organic totality', whose identity is not merely abstract (*SPR* 466, 468) : spirit, the universal element, lives and works in each citizen. Each particular member of the people, therefore, immediately and intuitively sees himself as identical with the universal, the absolute *Sittlichkeit* : in obeying the will of the people, he is obeying his own will.

Hegel differentiates three aspects of ethical life : absolute ethical life, relative ethical life and the ethical life of confidence. Absolute ethical life resides in a people (*SPR* 469–72). A people achieves recognition and verification of its identity, its individuality, in a war with an enemy people. Hegel points out that war is not a question of personal hatred and antagonisms; it is a war of a people against a people, 'free from all personal factors' (*SPR* 471). Absolute ethical life gives rise in the individual to the supreme virtue, encompassing all the other virtues : gallantry.

Besides the sphere of absolute ethical life there is the sphere of relative ethical life (*SPR* 472–3), which concerns relations between individuals. This is the realm of right. Right consists of guaranteeing that everyone will receive his due, by husbanding the resources of all the citizens and alleviating particular hardships. Unlike the sphere of absolute ethical life, the sphere of right is incapable of persuading the citizens to sacrifice their lives for the state. The virtue that corresponds to right is probity or honesty (*Rechtschaffenheit*).

Finally, apart from absolute ethical life and relative ethical life, Hegel distinguishes a third form of ethical life : the ethics of trust (*Zutrauen*) (*SPR* 473). Simple citizens, with their vulgar or common intuition, grasp the full value of absolute ethical life by means of their instinctive confidence in the overall organisation and fate of the world.

The different levels of ethical life just enumerated are embodied in several social classes. To absolute ethical life corresponds the absolute class (*absolute Stand*) (*SPR* 475–7), the proper task of which consists of satisfying not its own needs but those of the community; the essential function of this absolute class is to wage war. Since the absolute class is forbidden to look to its own material needs, it falls to the other classes to satisfy them.

To relative ethical life corresponds the class of probity or honesty (*Stand der Rechtschaffenheit*) (*SPR* 477–80), whose function it is to satisfy the material needs of the community through work, secure goods and constitute property. The value of the products of this activity is determined by the total system of needs of the community. The community develops money as a standard of exchange; and a system of exchange for the fruits of its labour. This is the system of commerce. Transfers of property from one proprietor to another and decisions concerning legitimate ownership of property are regulated by justice. Since violations of this justice are violations of the interests of a particular individual and not the interests of the whole nation, the appropriate sanctions are not vengeance or war but punishment. The living totality for the class of probity is not the people but the family and its ultimate aim is the acquisition of enough goods to ensure the continued existence of the family and a suitable education for the children. The class of probity or the 'bourgeois' class (*SPR* 477) is incapable of virtue; especially of the supreme virtue, gallantry. The highest degree of virtue to which it can aspire is its voluntary contribution towards the material needs of the absolute class and the assistance it renders to the destitute.

Finally, to the ethics of confidence corresponds the peasantry (*der Bauernstand*) (*SPR* 480). Their work is not creative : they do not destroy the objects of nature and then transform them, but they place their complete trust in the creative powers of nature itself. They do not concern themselves with right; and the property disputes that arise between members of this third class are resolved, not by tribunals, but through arbitration, which is itself an act of confidence in universal justice. Just as its own morality consists in its confidence in the superiority of the absolute class, it is itself capable of gallantry (unlike the class of relative morality); and it joins with the first class (as its foot-soldiers) for the defence of the community.

Hegel goes on to consider the development of modern society

under three headings: the system of needs; the system of justice (*Gerechtigkeit*); and the system of discipline (*Zucht*). These aspects of modern society correspond to the three moments of civil society discussed later by Hegel in the *Philosophy of Right*: the system of needs; the administration of justice; and finally, the public authority (*Polizei*) and the corporations. It is fascinating to see how deep an understanding Hegel had of the forces at work in modern society, at this early stage in his philosophical career. As we shall see, his main concern here is the polarity of wealth and poverty in modern industrial society and the concomitant estrangement of the individual members of the society from the community in which they live. This is precisely the kind of 'bifurcation' which prompted Hegel to turn to philosophy. We must ask ourselves how successful he is in mediating these bifurcations, in the manuscripts of the Jena period.

In earlier times, each man laboured to satisfy his own personal needs. As human consciousness developed, however, and needs multiplied, satisfaction of all those needs and desires became impossible for the individual. This has prompted the increasing division of labour: 'Labour, which relates to the object as a whole, is divided up and becomes individual labour; and precisely in this way, this individual labour becomes increasingly more mechanical' (*SPR* 437). In modern times, production for personal use has begun to give way to the mechanical production of surplus goods for exchange. There has arisen a system of 'completely quantitative and repetitive labour'; within this system of 'deadening mechanical labour', the individual labourer has lost touch with the product of his own labour (*SPR* 437). Production of objects for the personal use of the producer has been transformed into the production of commodities destined for the market, which is in turn regulated by a system of exchange value, money, prices and contract.

The system of needs is seen by Hegel as a 'system of universal mutual physical dependence' (*SPR* 492). But this system of inter-dependence among producers and consumers—the market mechanism—develops a dynamic of its own and comes to tyrannise the individual participants in the system: 'Nobody is self-sufficient regarding the totality of his needs. One's work . . . does not guarantee their satisfaction. [The system of needs] is an alien power, over which one has no control and upon which one is dependent' (*SPR* 492). The economic system is described by Hegel as an 'unconscious, blind fate' (*SPR* 493). The major factor in the impotence of the individual worker is the constant variability of the value of the products of his labour : 'This value itself is contingent on the sum total of needs and the sum total of the surplus; and this sum total is an almost indiscernible, invisible and unpredictable force' (*SPR* 492).

This system of interdependence which characterises modern industrial society, then, is ultimately anarchic, with no rational influence at the helm of the society to guide it. What determines the course of the society, on the contrary, is 'the unconscious blind totality of needs and the means of their satisfaction' (*SPR* 493). Men with a yearning for social integration must overcome their 'unconscious and blind fate' and institute some form of government whose primary function will be to tame the monster which men themselves have created. The government must intervene, to determine what a person needs at a certain time and place, in the wake of fluctuations in the value of labour.

Such intervention, however, is inadequate as long as the general anarchy of interests remains dominant in the society. In any case, says Hegel, such are the 'natural' inequalities of 'power' that gross inequalities are inevitable. The market mechanism merely exacerbates the inequalities engendered by the differences between the naturally well-endowed and the less well-endowed : 'This necessary inequality engenders . . . a relationship of domination' (*SPR* 495). The poor—those who do not own productive property—are thereby mercilessly pushed into a position of 'total physical dependence' upon 'the vastly wealthy individual' who owns the property and employs them (*SPR* 495). 'Great wealth is . . . bound up with extreme poverty' (*SPR* 496). In the process of economic development, that class of the population that is 'sacrificed to mechanical labour in factories' (*SPR* 496)—what Hegel calls 'the working class [*die arbeitende Klasse*]' (*SPR* 498)—is condemned to live 'in a brutal state' (*SPR* 496).

Hegel is at pains to point out that this extreme (and increasing) poverty is not accidental, but is endemic to modern civil society : 'This inequality of wealth is in and for itself necessary', since wealth has a necessary inherent tendency to accumulate ad infinitum (*ins Unendliche*) (*SPR* 495). The attempt by mankind to free itself from the fetters of need, by means of increasingly specialised production, has backfired in the most horrible way, with the creation of a monstrous system of commodity production which forces those who labour to live in the most dehumanising (and unfree) condition; and which serves to deepen the social and personal fragmentation of modern society.

In an attempt to overcome the antagonisms of the system of needs, Hegel goes on to describe a 'system of justice'. The system of justice represents the classical liberal view of government as simply a referee between conflicting property interests. The administrator of justice is not at all interested in individuals; he is only concerned with the acquisition, possession and exchange of goods, considered as a purely abstract process, and administers the law with 'complete indifference to any connection between the thing in question and this particular individual's need' (*SPR* 499). Judges approach particular cases as abstract exercises in the law of equity, with no overall view of the living totality of things and people. The system of justice, therefore, is interested in harmonising the antagonisms of civil society in the law courts only. Its 'principle of freedom' applies only to 'the analysis of legal disputes and rulings on them' (*SPR* 501).

Hegel finally seeks harmony among the conflicting interests in the system of discipline (*Zucht*). He will later expand on this under the heading of the public authority (*Polizei*). But here he limits himself to four aspects of the discipline of a people : public and private education, the cultural formation of the people which will lift up their souls to the worship of the truth; the straightforward 'law and order' disciplining of delinquent individuals by the police; the discipline exercised by 'the general ethical life [*Sittlichkeit*]'; and the formation of warriors, who will show their true value in the heat of battle (*SPR* 502).

There are some general points we can take from the 'System der Sittlichkeit' concerning the way in which Hegel proposes to give a philosophical account of social, political and economic phenomena. First, social and political experience is seen as an integral aspect of the development of the human spirit in history. Second—and I think this is the most important point—we can see how Hegel has assimilated the lessons he has learnt from Steuart and Schiller, concerning historical development. This consideration will be extremely important when we come to examine the *Philosophy of Right*.

In his mature social and political philosophy, Hegel divides

Sittlichkeit into three stages or aspects: the unmediated unity of family life; the selfish endeavours of individuals in civil society; and the self-conscious unity of the state (*PR* §157). If we can use Hegelian terminology for a moment, this is a development from unreflective universality to particularity and back to a higher universality. To use the more familiar terms we have been using in this book, Hegel is describing a development from primeval social harmony to modern fragmentation and back to harmony. Now, I have claimed that Hegel was desperately seeking social harmony. One might be tempted to look for that harmony in the direction of the family, as the most closely-knit social unit; since, as Hegel himself says, 'the family, as the immediate substantiality of spirit [*Geist*], is specifically characterised by love, which is mind's feeling of its own unity [*seine sich empfindende Einheit*]' (*PR* §158).

The fact that this unity is only *felt*, of course, and not understood rationally, is the crucial deficiency of family life. This 'immediate substantiality' may have been an appropriate form of human association in earlier epochs; but it has been superseded by modern Man's awareness of his own individual freedom. 'This substantiality [of family life] loses its unity,' says Hegel, 'passes over into bifurcation [*Entzweiung*], and into the phase of relation, i.e. into *Civil Society*' (*PR* §157). The unmediated harmony of the *natürliche Sittlichkeit* has been shattered, according to Hegel, by the emergence of self-consciousness in the labour process; this developing labour process he describes, in the *Philosophy of Right*, under the heading of 'civil society'. Furthermore, there is no point at all, at this stage in history, in hankering after the old form of social coherence. The free individual has become the dominant force in history; and instead of harking back to the old days of unreflective community, a new rational spirit of community must be inspired among the free, self-conscious individuals of the modern world. When we come to examine the *Philosophy of Right* in detail, therefore, we shall not concern ourselves with Hegel's analysis of family life. Rather, we shall concentrate on Hegel's description of civil society—'the achievement of the modern world' (*PR* §182A) —and his attempts to weld the mutually antagonistic 'self-subsistent individuals [*selbständiger Einzelner*]' (*PR* §157) of civil society into a rational, harmonious state. Our examination of civil society will demonstrate the magnitude of Hegel's task. When we come to examine his agencies of mediation, we shall then be in a position to inquire whether or not he has succeeded.

Already in the 'System der Sittlichkeit', Hegel gives a vivid account of the stage in the labour process which has been reached in modern, commodity-producing society. In this, he demonstrates his familiarity with the dynamics of an economic system which was already firmly entrenched in Great Britain and, to a lesser extent, in France, but which had not yet developed in Germany. Hegel does not flinch from drawing attention to those facets of this economic system which threaten to get out of control. The economic life of the community—the aspect of human organisation which he was later to call 'civil society'—must, therefore, be regulated by the state. If understood philosophically—as part of the rational development of the human spirit—this regulation by the state will be seen not as an infringement on the freedom of the individual members of civil society, but as a means of safeguarding and promoting that freedom.

In all his subsequent writings on political and social matters, Hegel demonstrates a profound awareness of the dire conditions in which many people actually live in the modern state. Before turning to the *Philosophy of Right*, I would like briefly to consider the sociological descriptions of modern commodity-producing society which he offers in his Jena lectures on the philosophy of spirit (1803–6).

The Realphilosophie : *Alienated Labour*

The evolution of modern commercial and industrial society from the earliest forms of 'immediate' community proceeds in these lectures in much the same fashion as it had done in the 'System der Sittlichkeit'. The development of self-consciousness and mutual recognition is brought about through the medium of labour, a rational and distinctively human rather than an instinctual or merely animalistic activity : 'Labour is not an instinct, but a function of reason which develops into a universal in the people; and as such it is contrary to the particularity of the individual, which must be overcome' (*JR* I, 236). Furthermore, as tools are invented by individuals, their invention is recognised and mastered by others; becomes used throughout the community 'and immediately becomes common property' (*JR* I, 237). Here Hegel is highlighting the role of labour and the development of primitive technology as a positive force in history.

He then proceeds to analyse the correlation between increasing mechanisation and the increasing alienation of the worker from his labour. Machines mean less work for the society, but not for individuals; because more of the work that had formerly required direct human labour can now be done by machines, workers are not indispensable as they once were and the value of their work falls correspondingly: 'In the machine, Man terminates his own formal activity and lets it do all the work for him . . . The more mechanical labour becomes, the less value it has and the more [the worker] has to work in this manner' (*JR* I, 237).

In a typically Hegelian manner, Hegel points to both the good aspect and the bad aspect of mechanisation and the parallel division of labour. On the one hand, the division of labour means that each individual is dependent on many other individuals for the satisfaction of his needs. This is an integrating characteristic of the division of labour: 'Man no longer acquires by working what he needs, nor does he any longer need what he has produced. . . . His labour becomes formal, abstract, universal, discrete; he restricts himself to working to satisfy one of his own needs and exchanges the product of this labour for what is necessary for the satisfaction of his other needs' (*JR* I, 238). The system of needs is an advance towards community from the earlier stage of isolated individual labour: 'The satisfaction of needs is a system of universal dependence of everyone on each other' (*JR* I, 238). Furthermore, workers are now emancipated from their dependence on Nature; and their comfort increases.

On the other hand, however, this 'abstract' labour produces a gulf between the individual and the complete satisfaction of his own needs. He is no longer self-sufficient: 'There disappears for everyone all sense of security and certainty that his individual labour is immediately adequate to his needs' (*JR* I, 238). Not only is he no longer self-sufficient, but he is totally at the mercy of a system of exchange over which he has absolutely no control. As mechanisation and specialisation of skills increase, the individual is rendered less capable of fending for himself: 'Labour becomes more and more dead absolutely, it becomes mechanical work. The skill of the individual worker becomes all the more limited, to an infinite degree, and the consciousness of the factory worker is degraded to the ultimate state of dullness' (*JR* I, 239).

The balance between the sum of needs and the totality of goods produced to satisfy those needs is a delicate one : it becomes 'a completely incalculable and blind dependence' (*JR* I, 239). Workers depend for the satisfaction of their needs upon their own ability to produce goods, for which they receive wages : 'a distant transaction can often suddenly impede the work of a whole class [*Klasse*] of people, who satisfy their needs with it; and thus render their labour superfluous and useless' (*JR* I, 239). These workers can, thus, be suddenly thrown out of work and deprived of the very wages which they need to satisfy their needs.

In the earlier lectures (1804), Hegel summed up the precarious nature of the interdependence characteristic of modern commodity-producing society thus : 'If need and labour are elevated to the universality [of a money economy], there emerges in a great people a vast system of solidarity [*Gemeinschaftlichkeit*] and mutual dependence, a life of the dead with its own momentum [*ein sich in sich bewegendes Leben des Toten*]; this system moves hither and thither blindly and primitively in its agitation and, like a wild animal, demands constant strict control and restraint' (*JR* I, 240). Hegel went on to elaborate on the form this 'strict control and restraint' might take in his second set of lectures a year or two later. There, however, he describes the 'wild animal' of modern industrial society in even more passionate terms than in *Realphilosophie I*.

Once more, he refers to the stultifying effects of machine-labour : 'Because of the abstraction of labour, [the worker] becomes more mechanical, more deadened and more mindless. . . . The strength of the self consists of its rich comprehensiveness; this is lost' (*JR* II, 232). Hegel is convinced, furthermore, that the dehumanising life of drudgery and destitution inflicted on the people who man the machines is not merely a contingent and infrequent by-product of the factory system; it is, on the contrary, a necessary corollary of the wealth accruing to the owners of the machines : 'A multitude is condemned to a brutal and stupefying condition in labour and poverty, so that others might amass wealth' (*JR* II, 238). 'This is the spirit of complete mercilessness', inherent in a society dominated by exchange through the medium of money, in which 'currency must be honoured, but family, welfare, life etc. may all perish' (*JR* II, 257).

One can feel the indignation in his words (reminiscent of his strictures on private property during his tenure in Bern), when Hegel describes the class-domination upon which modern society depends for its prosperity : 'Factories, manufacturing works depend for their very existence on the misery of a class [*Klasse*]'—the class of industrial workers (*JR* II, 257). Hegel describes the human effects of the factory system of mass production : 'Masses of the population are condemned to labour in factories, manufacturing works, mines, etc.; work which is totally stupefying, unhealthy, insecure and faculty-stunting' (*JR* II, 232).

As if these working conditions are not bad enough, those who work in them are dependent on the vagaries of an unpredictable economic system over which they have absolutely no control : 'Branches of industry which supported an entire class [*Klasse*] of people suddenly collapse because of [changes in] fashion or because of a drop in prices due to discoveries in other countries, etc.; and this whole mass of people are abandoned to helpless poverty. The contrast between vast wealth and vast poverty appears; poverty which cannot help itself in any way' (*JR* II, 232). Once again, Hegel insists that this polarisation of economic inequality is endemic to the system. He demonstrates most forcibly that he has a clear conception—in embryonic form, at least—of what later came to be known as the accumulation of capital. 'Wealth . . . transforms itself into a power. The accumulation of wealth takes place partly by chance, partly through the universality of distribution. Wealth is a kind of magnet. . . . It collects other wealth around itself, just as a large mass attracts smaller masses to itself. Whoever has, to him will it be given [*Wer da hat, dem wird gegeben*]' (*JR* II, 232-3). In other words, money makes money. 'Acquisition becomes a manifold system which invests on all sides into areas in which a smaller business cannot profit' (*JR* II, 233).

Hegel concludes his terrifying picture of the anarchy of civil society on a warning note : 'This disparity between wealth and poverty, this need and necessity, results in the utmost laceration of the human will, in inner resentment and hatred' (*JR* II, 233). The multiplex fragmentation—of the personality and of society—which had prompted Hegel to write a philosophical account of human experience in the first place, is accentuated, as never before, by the conditions of wage-labour in factories and by the extremes of wealth and poverty endemic to modern civil society.

Much of the description of the dynamics and actual conditions of modern industrial society which Hegel offers in these social and political writings of the Jena period reappears—in a more philosophical (and often simply more obscure) form—in the 'civil society' section of the *Philosophy of Right* (1821). Before we go on to examine the *Philosophy of Right*, however, we might pause briefly to consider just how amazing it is that Hegel—writing in a German university town, in the first few years of the nineteenth century—should offer such a brilliant and penetrating analysis of modern industrial society. In doing so, we might also attempt to clarify Hegel's relation to political economy.

Hegel's Sources: Newspapers and the Political Economists

The first thing that is clear is that Hegel's model was not a German one. As we saw when we examined 'The German Constitution', there were hardly any factories or textile mills in Germany at the beginning of the nineteenth century. Consequently, there were practically no social evils and conflicts of the kind Hegel describes in connection with the capitalist economy. In fact, as we pointed out earlier, Germany was just emerging from a feudal economic system—serfdom was still to be abolished in Prussia, in 1807—and the principal conflicts to come in Germany were to be between an emerging class of industrialists, merchants and financiers (Hegel's *Stand des Gewerbes*) and the rearguard action of the old autocratic-oligarchic order. Germany—unlike France and Great Britain—had yet to have its 'bourgeois revolution'. Industry was still at a relatively early stage of development in France; Hegel's sources, therefore, were obviously British.

In Britain, a class-conscious capitalism had developed rapidly in the eighteenth century, bringing about increasing industrialisation and urbanisation. This brought in its wake a new form of mass suffering and debilitation : widespread poverty. The spectacle of hunger and need was not new, of course. But the growth of huge urban armies of people afflicted by an epidemic of poverty, which they were helpless to cure, was a new and terrifying phenomenon.

There is plenty of evidence that Hegel had studied the political economy of Ferguson, Steuart and Adam Smith (1723–90).[2] Hegel, however, could not possibly have derived from their rather academic studies of economic theory the vivid canvas he paints of human degradation in the factory mode of production. It is extremely likely that Hegel arrived at his own analysis by supplementing his study of the political economists with his constant reading of English newspapers and journals. These publications would have carried long and detailed reports of social conditions in Britain; and reports of parliamentary debates on the Poor Laws, the first Factory Act of 1802, and other new legislation.

I have been at great pains to emphasise Hegel's intense everyday interest in political matters. So interested was he that he agreed to take a job as editor of a pro-French newspaper in Bamberg (Bavaria), shortly after his departure from Jena; he speaks of it enthusiastically in a letter written on 20 February 1807 : 'The work itself will interest me since, as you yourself know, I follow world affairs with curiosity' (*BH* I, 145). To a friend he confides that 'as you know, I always had a passion for politics' (30 August 1807) (*BH* I, 186). His avid newspaper-reading dates from his early student days in Tübingen. Much later, Hegel spoke with enthusiasm of this method of keeping closely in touch with the world around him : 'I still take delight . . . especially in my power and passion for newspaper reading' (21 February 1815) (*BH* II, 50).

Hegel, then, depended on his own reading of journalistic reports for the concrete details of his description of factory labour. But the general framework of his discussion was provided by the political economists—primarily Steuart and Smith. This, in itself, offers an interesting clash between two ways of viewing the market economy : between the pessimist and the optimist, so to speak. Steuart had alerted Hegel to the fragile nature of the balance between supply and demand in a money economy. The state must constantly guard against the inherent instability of the economy, according to Steuart, by regulating the transactions of the market. And it was in Steuart that Hegel encountered the figure of the statesman, curbing the wild animal that threatens at any time to go completely out of control.

If Steuart highlights the irrational aspects of commodity-producing society, Smith, on the other hand, emphasises the 'show of rationality [*Scheinen der Vernünftigkeit*]' (*PR* §189) running through the market economy, which makes a science of political economy possible. The economy, according to Smith, is self-regulating. If the state does not intervene in the mechanism of the market economy, an 'invisible hand' will see to it that each member of the community shares in the total wealth produced. What is remarkable is that Hegel, while accepting the elements of truth contained in Smith's schema, managed to resist the attraction of the over-optimistic dogma of laissez-faire, which had become dominant in German economic circles around the turn of the century. Steuart's warnings about the instability of the money economy—supported by Hegel's own investigations—prompted him to reject the complacency of Smith's doctrine and align himself with a long German tradition of governmental control of economic life, represented chiefly by Justi and the Cameralists and (as late as 1800) Fichte's *Closed Commercial State*.

The Philosophy of Right:
The Rational State

Social Labour and Private Property

The *Philosophy of Right* can be thought of as describing the progress of the human will through various stages to the conscious actualised freedom of man as a member of the social order. (It is, perhaps, more Hegelian to consider these stages as various *levels* of the will's consciousness of its freedom, rather than as a temporal or historical progression; but it is undeniable that the work does have a readily-discernible historical dimension.) There are three main stages or levels: (1) Abstract right—in which the will is immediate (not yet mediated by other people) and right is merely abstract or formal; (2) Morality (*Moralität*)—in which the will is reflective or conscious of itself, but morality is still purely subjective and untouched by social conditions; (3) Ethical life (*Sittlichkeit*)— in which self-conscious right is applied to the social realm and freedom becomes a practical reality in the world (in Hegelian terminology, freedom is actualised).

'Ethical life' itself has three aspects or levels: (a) The Family— ethical life in its immediate, relatively unreflective phase in which pristine universality is present, but in an unconscious (and therefore inadequate) manner; (b) Civil society—in which subjective particularity (i.e. individual freedom) is actualised and consciousness comes to play an important role in the multiplication and satisfaction of human needs. Individuals become more and more conscious of their interdependence until civil society is subsumed into (c) The State —in which the universality implicit in civil society is actualised, without violating subjective freedom.[1]

Hegel's definition of civil society (*bürgerliche Gesellschaft*) clearly follows the model of the free market in which it is 'every man for himself' and a Smithian 'invisible hand' ensures that all will turn out for the best: 'Civil society—an association of members as self-subsistent [i.e. autonomous] individuals in a universality which, because of their self-subsistence, is only abstract. Their association is brought about by their needs, by the legal system—the means to security of person and property—and by an external organisation for attaining their particular and common interests' (§157).

Unlike the spheres of the abstract and the isolated subject, civil society—'the achievement of the modern world' (§182A)—is the sphere of the 'concrete person, who is himself the object of his particular aims' (§182). Civil society is the *bellum omnium contra omnes* : 'the battlefield where everyone's individual private interest meets everyone else's' (§289R), where each self-seeking individual is totally absorbed in satisfying his own selfish needs. Civil society is also, however, a process of mediation of particularity. Each individual comes to realise how closely he is related to all the other individuals; the pursuit of private ends (Hegel's 'particularity') turns out to be governed by the universal laws of political economy. The universality of these laws, which is 'reason glinting through' the selfishness (§182A), gradually asserts itself until the universal, which has hitherto been implicit, becomes explicit in the state.

Individuals come to see how 'the livelihood, happiness, and legal status of one man is interwoven with the livelihood, happiness, and rights of all' (§183). But the resultant 'system of complete interdependence' (§183) is used as a *means* to selfish ends, not as an end in itself. As a result, social relationships within civil society are reduced to relationships between individuals with needs and other individuals who are merely means to their satisfaction (§182A). The 'universal' (i.e. the community) is still seen as something distinct from, alien from, the particular individual in this 'external state, the state based on need' (§183). The universal and the particular will only be synthesised when the former comes to be internalised in the consciousness of individuals, in the state proper.

Hegel admits that 'in civil society universal and particular have fallen apart' (§184A). In other words, free individuals are so intent on pursuing their own private, selfish ends that they have lost all respect for the common good. This prompts Hegel's first statement of the economic problem which will concern him throughout his account of civil society : 'civil society affords the spectacle of extravagance and want as well as of the physical and ethical degeneration common to them both' (§185). This theme will recur time and again : it is a fundamental characteristic of civil society, says Hegel, that it will produce extremes of wealth and want.

He explains that the solution suggested by Plato for this problem of economic polarity—the complete exclusion of subjective freedom from the state and denial of private property, family life, choice of social position etc. (which would be an easy way out)—is unacceptable, because 'the principle of the self-subsistent, inherently infinite personality of the individual, the principle of subjective freedom, is denied its right' in Plato's ideal republic (§185R).

So this is Hegel's dilemma. The rational modern state must allow freedom to the particular person. But 'particularity by itself is measureless excess' (§185A); it must be mediated. The state must be strong enough to 'put particularity in harmony with the unity of ethical life' (§185A). It must manage to resolve the tension between expanding desires and expanding want and destitution (§185A).

Civil society contains three stages or aspects : (a) the system of needs; (b) the administration of justice; (c) the public authority (*Polizei*) and corporations (§188). Hegel's account of the expansion of human needs and desires in civil society is very important for his analysis of the emergence of widespread poverty. In the system of needs, the understanding[2]—although a mere 'show of rationality' (§189) appropriate to this stage in the development of the human mind—effects the reconciliation of subjective needs and objective satisfaction by means of external objects, labour and effort. Men and conditions may vary, but every man needs food, drink, clothing, and so on (§189A). These needs are universal to all members of civil society, to each individual burgher or *bourgeois* (§190R). Furthermore, a vital aspect of man's being conscious is his ability to transcend his basic animal needs (§185A).

The understanding multiplies needs and the means to satisfy them (§190, §190A), then discriminates among these multiplied needs and passes judgment on the suitability of means (§191). A simple (and silly) example may serve to illustrate the kind of process that Hegel is thinking about. We can imagine two farmers who have hitherto been totally self-subsistent, satisfying the needs of their respective families (this would correspond to the moment of the Family or Clan in ethical life). Farmer Smith found that he could grow fruit plentifully on his land, but that he could not produce vegetables. Farmer Jones had the kind of soil that produced excellent vegetables, but no fruit. They had never really thought about their respective deficiencies before. But once they became aware of the riches in the other man's field, they came to *need* them. So, they decided to exchange the products of their labour. There then arose the problem of transporting the fruit and vegetables. For the first time, these men *needed* a means of transportation. One can imagine that these were the kinds of circumstances that prompted Man to invent the wheel. Thus, human needs multiply ad infinitum.

In this process, 'needs and means become abstract in quality' (§192) : i.e. they come to be considered as elements in a simple economic model of production and consumption. Needs and means constitute the basis of the reciprocal relations among individuals : 'We play into each other's hands and so hang together. To this extent everything private becomes something social' (§192A). Furthermore, the use of intelligence liberates people from mere natural needs into the realm of *social* needs, 'the conjunction of immediate or natural needs with mental needs arising from ideas' (§194). This transition from the natural and private to the mental and social is evidence, for Hegel, of the gradual reintegration of modern society : the universal is gradually asserting itself, albeit implicitly.

A corollary of this growing primacy of ideas and opinions, along with emerging social consciousness, is the growing demand for equality of satisfaction with others : emulation becomes 'a fruitful source of the multiplication of needs and their expansion' (§193). Already in his *Realphilosophie*, Hegel had written at length on the importance of 'fashion, fickleness and freedom' in the development of needs (*JR* II, 231–2). In this analysis, he puts his finger on a phenomenon which motivational psychologists only clearly identified some twenty years ago[3] and which is used to great effect in advertising pitches such as the recent TV slogan for selling motor cars : 'Will your next car be a step up for you?' And indeed, in an extremely perceptive prophecy and critique of the modern advertising industry, Hegel remarks in passing that 'the need for greater comfort does not exactly arise within you directly; it is suggested to you by those who hope to make a profit from its creation' (§191A).[4]

This multiplication of needs, means and enjoyments leads, on the one hand, to luxury. 'In this same process, however, dependence and want increase ad infinitum (§195). . . . When luxury is at its height, distress and depravity are equally extreme' (§195A). It is important to note that this tendency to economic polarisation is presented as a *law* of political economy: it is not a contingent aspect of civil society but inherent in it.

Furthermore, because private property is 'the *embodiment* of personality' (§51) for Hegel, and the right of private property is inviolable, 'the material to meet [dependence and want] is permanently barred to the needy man because it consists of external objects with the special character of being property, the embodiment of the free will of others, and hence from his point of view its recalcitrance is absolute' (§195). In other words, the means of satisfying his needs are absolutely inaccessible to the propertyless man, because he has not the medium of exchange—money—with which to purchase them; and to avail himself of them without payment would be stealing, an intolerable offence in civil society where private property is sacrosanct. This is the first explicit statement in the *Philosophy of Right* of the plight of the people of no property in civil society; and Hegel acknowledges already the inevitability of that plight.

The Division of Labour and Social Classes

What Hegel calls the 'cunning of reason', however (*List der Vernunft*), is at work. 'By a dialectical advance,' says Hegel, 'subjective self-seeking turns into a contribution to the satisfaction of the needs of everyone else . . . with the result that each man in earning, producing, and enjoying on his own account is *eo ipso* producing and earning for the enjoyment of everyone else' (§199). Hegel has previously pointed out that an element of universality inevitably emerges from the dynamics of civil society (§189R, §197A); the workings of the free market do produce interaction and interdependence among individuals (§199). But now he seems to be going a step further and accepting the Smithian idea that, in this interdependence, the needs of *all* the people are inevitably being satisfied.

Well, Hegel does qualify this somewhat over-optimistic generalisation when he remarks that a particular individual's opportunities to share in the common resource are conditioned 'partly by his own unearned principal (his capital [*Kapital*]), and partly by his skill' (§200). A person cannot engage in any dealings with the common pool of resources (*Vermögen*) unless he has some resources[5] of his own which he can exchange; or a skill, so that he can work and earn a living (§199). But many people in civil society have not the wherewithal—neither in terms of *Vermögen* nor *Kapital*—to share in the benefits of the wealth generated by the community; and the individual's skill is in turn dependent 'not only on his capital, but also on accidental circumstances' which affect bodily and mental development (§200).

This is another of Hegel's remarkably modern insights, this time into differences in educational achievement (foreseeing contemporary findings about the effects of economic and social environment, chronic malnutrition, etc. on intellectual capacities).[6] He starts from the conviction that 'men are made unequal by nature' (§200R);[7] and instead of being mitigated in civil society, these inequalities are compounded. 'Disparities of individual resources [*Vermögen*] and ability'—physical and intellectual, financial and moral—are the 'inevitable consequence' (§200). And the victims of these disparities are effectively excluded from the benefits of the general resources of the society. This would appear to be a serious shortcoming in a society that is supposed to be reciprocally beneficial to all its members.

'The infinitely complex, criss-cross, movements of reciprocal production and exchange, and the equally infinite multiplicity of means therein employed' cause the members of civil society to form themselves into general groups (§201). Hegel names these classes or estates [*Stände*] as (a) the 'immediate' agricultural class, (b) the 'reflecting' business class, and (c) the 'universal' class of public servants (§202).

The important characteristic of the agricultural class is that, while its members do possess private property, their mode of production is relatively unreflective and depends more on the caprice of nature (e.g. the seasons, the climate) than on the intelligence (§203A). Hegel remarks, however, in another of his prophetic insights, that agriculture in his day is becoming increasingly like industry : farms are being run like factories (§203A). Hegel seems to be aware of the process whereby developments such as increased mechanisation mean that more intensive competition among farmers forces the smaller farmers, who have not the means to buy costly machinery, to sell their holdings and become wage labourers : they either remain in the countryside to work as wage-earning farm labourers for the new entrepreneurial farmers, or they go to the cities and towns to swell the ranks of the urban working class.

The business class (*Stand des Gewerbes*) is the prime example of men using their intelligence to master nature and satisfy their needs. This class is involved in three levels of activity (corresponding to the increasing integration of society) : (a) craftsmanship, or relatively concrete labour; (b) manufacture, or labour of a more abstract nature, whereby mass-production satisfies more universal demands; (c) trade, 'the business of exchange, whereby separate utilities are exchanged the one for the other', through the use of money (and, we might add, stocks and shares and suchlike means), 'which actualises the abstract value of all commodities' (§204).

It is not clear whether Hegel wishes to include the people who actually work for wages in factories in the manufacturing class (*Fabrikantenstand*) (§204) or whether he means this latter class to be made up solely of entrepreneurs, the *owners* of the means of manufacture. In his *Realphilosophie II*, he had identified two main sub-classes within the class of business (*Gewerbe*) : the burgher or artisan class (*Bürgerstand*) and the merchant class (*Kaufmannsstand*). He mentioned another sub-class, however, when he wrote that 'factories, manufacturing works depend for their very existence on the misery of a class [*Klasse*]' (*JR* II, 257). It is not at all clear whether, in the *Philosophy of Right*, the working *Klasse* has become part of the manufacturing class, the *Fabrikantenstand*. This issue will be very important later when we come to consider Hegel's mediations and the position of the working class and the unemployable 'rabble' (*Pöbel*) vis-à-vis the corporations and the state. We might note here, however, that whatever about the status of the working class, there is no place at all in this neat schema of need-satisfaction for the unemployed, those masses displaced from the cycle of production by the development of technology.

Law as the Arbiter of Private Interests

The Administration of Justice is the second of the three moments of Hegel's civil society. It is important to remember that this moment is not incompatible with the System of Needs : they are both coexisting aspects of civil society. The Administration of Justice attempts to mitigate some of the hardships in the System of Needs. But the polarising tendencies of free enterprise still prevail. Whereas in the System of Needs right was merely *abstract* as the interdependence and reciprocity of needs and means, right now

D

becomes *concrete* in society, becomes 'universally recognised, known and willed' (§209), acquires power and thereby becomes known as 'universally valid' (§210) through the administration of justice. This is the realm of universal human rights, in which 'a man counts as a man in virtue of his manhood alone, not because he is a Jew, Catholic, Protestant, German, Italian, etc.' (§209R). There follows an extended disquisition on the advantages of legal codification over mere customary or English common law. Legal codification is not a question of inventing laws in a vacuum, but of codifying or making *universal* already existing laws and customs. The important thing is not that the laws in the modern state are written down, but that 'knowledge of the content of the law in its determinate universality' is available to *all* the members of the civil society (§211R).

Continuing in this vein, he emphasises that if laws are to be binding they must be made readily available to all, in clearly-understood terminology : 'to hang the laws so high that no citizen could read them' is just as serious an injustice against self-consciousness as burying them in legal tomes written in Latin (§215R). Hegel criticises the legal profession for refusing to allow laymen to discuss law and claiming a monopoly on legal know-how : if a man is denied knowledge of the law, he argues, he has no obligation to obey it (§215A). 'At one time,' says Hegel, the administration of justice was 'turned into an instrument of profit and tyranny, when the knowledge of the law was buried in pedantry and a foreign tongue, and knowledge of legal processes was similarly buried in involved formalities' (§297R). The clear implication is that this is no longer the case, in modern civil society.

Hegel's discussion of the Court of Justice is another good example of his continuing difficulty in maintaining a balance between private interests and universal rights. He insists that the courts are not mere historical accidents, but are in keeping with the progress of the Idea in history (§219R). He rejects the 'barbarous notion' that the administration of justice is 'an improper exercise of force, a suppression of freedom, and a despotism' (§219R). Such an assertion, he claims, is the crudest anarchy and advocates a free rein for rampant particularity.

Of course, Hegel is walking a tightrope here, because he himself sees the administration of justice as the means of safeguarding unfettered individual freedom in the economic sphere (§157) : 'the right of property is no longer merely implicit but has attained its recognised actuality as the protection of property through the administration of justice' (§208). At the same time, however, he must ensure, for the purposes of furthering the reintegration of modern society, that the judicial system 'vindicate itself as something universal' (§219).

One of the ways of ensuring this is to guarantee the right to a public trial, because 'a trial is implicitly an event of universal validity' (§224). Public proceedings are necessary, because 'an integral part of justice is the confidence which citizens have in it' (§224A) : citizens must be convinced that the judgment is actually just. Even so, if the criminal lies and does not confess his guilt, then the verdict of the judge will be seen both by him and by his fellow-citizens as something alien to him and as a denial of his subjectivity. The mediating term here is 'trial by jury, which meets the demand that the declaration of guilt or innocence shall spring from the soul of the accused' (§227A). Judgment by one's peers is a symbol of the universality of the administration of justice.

Hegel goes on to admit that this system of 'universal' justice is open to abuse. The 'right of self-consciousness' is violated if the law becomes inaccessible to any section of civil society. Knowledge of the law and access to the court may become 'the property of a class which makes itself an exclusive clique by the use of a terminology like a foreign tongue to those whose rights are at issue' (§228R). Should this happen, 'the members of civil society, who depend for their livelihood on their industry . . . are kept strangers to the law . . . and the result is that they become the wards, or even in a sense, the bondsmen, of the legal profession' (§228R).

This is a striking statement of the limitations of the system of universal justice in modern society : 'They [wage-earners] may indeed have the right to appear in court in person and to "stand" there (*in judicio stare*), but their bodily presence is a trifle if their minds are not to be there also, if they are not to follow the proceedings with their own knowledge, and if the justice they receive remains in their eyes a doom pronounced *ab extra*' (§228R). Hegel clearly implies—albeit grudgingly—that this is in fact what happens. And if it is possible that a wage-labourer (and it is almost universally the case) be present in court 'in body' only, then how much more is it the case for the 'rabble of paupers' that 'the justice they receive remains in their eyes a doom pronounced *ab extra*'?

Thus far in my account of civil society, I have endeavoured to be as concrete as possible and to avoid Hegel's confusing 'dialectical' terminology as far as possible. Now that I have described some of the dynamics of civil society, and now that (hopefully) a pattern of developments has emerged in Hegel's description, we may appreciate more fully his summing up of the development of civil society so far, using his own 'philosophical' language.

'In civil society,' he says, 'the Idea is lost in particularity and has fallen asunder with the separation of inward and outward' (§229). This refers to the system of needs, the earliest workings of the free enterprise economic system. 'The Idea' is the subject-matter of Hegel's philosophy—the totality of human experience—a segment of which he is purporting to describe in the *Philosophy of Right*. 'The Idea' is the all-encompassing synthesis of subject and object, of particularity and universality : for the purpose of this study of specifically social and political experience, 'the Idea' is the synthesis of the free individual and the community.

In civil society, with the unleashing of the forces of unfettered individualism, a gap appears between the two components of this synthesis. The free individual perceives the state as an alien power bent on restricting his freedom; he proceeds to indulge in an orgy of self-seeking activity in the economic field. This is an aspect of the fragmentation and dissonance which Hegel had experienced for many years in the world around him. The institutionalisation of the division of labour, however, fosters a general awareness of the mutual interdependence of the free individuals in civil society. And this realisation is the first stage of social integration.

This interdependence is further institutionalised in the legal system which governs property relations between free individuals : 'In the administration of justice . . . civil society returns to its concept, to the unity of the implicit universal with the subjective particular [i.e. the system of mutual interdependence], although here . . . the universality in question is that of *abstract* right' (§229). That is to say, the laws and the courts represent a form of integration *in theory* only. This theory must be given some muscle to make it workable; and there must be an institution with which free individuals can identify, and through which they can have their voice heard in the community.

'The actualisation of this unity [of the universal and the particular] through its extension to the whole ambit of particularity is (i) the specific function of the police [*Polizei*], though the unification which it effects is only relative; (ii) it is the corporation which actualises the unity completely, though only in a whole which, while concrete, is restricted' (§229). Complete and adequate unity of universality and particularity will, of course, only be made possible in the state. We can now examine the *Polizei* and the corporations—two of Hegel's most important mediating or integrating institutions—in more detail.

The Need for Solidarity: the Public Authority

It is clear from Hegel's treatment of the *Polizei* in his early writings that he uses the term to denote not just the police force, but a regulatory agency of supervision and control with a much wider brief : in fact, the term 'police' was commonly used in this sense of 'public authority' or 'civil administration' in the literature of Hegel's own day.[8]

Hegel says that he takes the term *Polizei* 'from the Greek term *politeia*, meaning civil life and government, the activities of the whole itself. Its reference is now [i.e. as applied to modern civil society] restricted to the activities of the whole in matters concerning public security of any kind, the supervision of business to prevent fraud. Through the public authority, universal trust is realised, e.g. trust in the exchange of commodities. . . . The public authority ensures that a contract will be honoured' (*JR* II, 259).

Hegel had viewed the modern state as an instrument for the protection of property even in his earliest writings : 'In the states of the modern era [what he now refers to as 'civil societies'], security of property is the axis on which all legislation turns, to which most rights of the citizen refer' (*DHE* 268). The justification he now offers for the public authority (*Polizei*) is twofold : (a) that the 'undisturbed safety of person and property be attained'; and (b) 'that the securing of every single person's livelihood and welfare be treated and actualised as a right' (§230).

'Police control and penal justice' are introduced because 'the actions of individuals may always be wrongful' (§233), i.e. the right to private property may be violated. Furthermore, 'there is no inherent line between what is and what is not injurious', suspicious, to be forbidden or submitted to surveillance (§234); this is determined by contingent factors, such as contemporary conditions. The 'universal activities and organisations of general utility' which call for the oversight of the public authority (§235) are those which ensure the smooth running of industry for the maximisation of profits (this is, after all, the whole *raison d'être* of civil society).

Hegel acknowledges that these activities may lead to conflicts : 'the differing interests of producers and consumers may come into collision with each other' (§236), to such an extent that police control may be necessary 'to diminish the danger of upheavals arising from clashing interests' (§236R). It is not clear what are the 'clashing interests' to which Hegel is referring. But his remarks in the *Realphilosophie II* suggest that he is talking about clashes between employers and employees : 'Factories, manufacturing works depend for their very existence on the misery of a class [*Klasse*, the working class]' (*JR* II, 257).

This economic inequality results in an explosive 'relationship of domination' (*SPR* 495). And 'if [legal and orderly] means are lacking' for representing the interests of the multitude through mediation, 'the voice of the masses is always for violence' (§302A).

Hegel has previously pointed out, quite explicitly, that civil society—at least, the system of needs—is the free play of competitive and mutually antagonistic free individuals; by its very nature, it is the *bellum omnium contra omnes*. Aware of the danger that these antagonisms might become accentuated to the pitch that civil society might tear itself apart—'the Idea . . . has fallen asunder' (§229)—he tries to mitigate as far as possible the effects of the 'contingencies on the subjective side' (§237) of civil society, for example, the fact that people are not born equal.

One of the ways in which he proposes to do this is through a programme of education : 'In its character as a universal family, civil society has the right and duty of superintending and influencing education, inasmuch as education bears upon the child's capacity to become a member of society. . . . To the same end, society must provide public educational facilities as far as is practicable' (§239). One of the primary motivations for this universal educational programme is to ensure that every member of civil society has a reasonable opportunity of becoming a member of the universal class, the state bureaucracy, devoted to the welfare of the entire community.

'The universal class has for its task the universal interests of the community' (§205). In performing this task, 'private interest finds its satisfaction in its work for the universal' (§205); the universal class is Hegel's paradigm of mediation between the particular and the universal. In keeping with its name, membership of Hegel's universal class is open to all : entrance depends on the candidate's 'knowledge and proof of ability. . . . Since it is the sole condition of appointment, [such proof] guarantees to every citizen the chance of joining the class of civil servants' (§291). In civil society, Hegel claims, in the matter of one's class in society 'the essential and final determining factors are subjective opinion and the individual's arbitrary will' (§206). He condemns Plato's Republic and the Indian caste-system, because in them the individual's social position is determined by the decision of the ruling class and an accident of birth respectively, thereby denying the principle of subjective particularity its rights (§206R).

Education is the open door to membership of the bureaucracy which stands above the sectional interests of civil society. Hegel continually stresses the importance of education in the mediating process within civil society : 'education bears on the child's capacity to become a member of a society' (§239).[9] Education liberates the individual from the snare of his own particularity by training him to use his intelligence and thereby focus on what is universal rather than idiosyncratic (§187) : 'the final purpose of education, therefore, is liberation' (§187R).[10] Hegel is all too aware, however, that education—or any other such means of integration—may not be capable of countering the negative aspects of civil society, of curbing 'the wild animal running hither and thither blindly and primitively' (*JR* I, 240).

The Problem of Poverty and Hegel's Solutions

One of the most striking negative aspects of civil society is the spread of poverty. The paragraph in which Hegel sums up much of what he had already said concerning poverty is worth quoting in its entirety :

> Not only caprice, however, but also contingencies, physical conditions, and factors grounded in external circumstances [see §200] may reduce men to poverty. The poor still have the needs common to civil society, and yet since society has withdrawn from them the natural means of acquisition [see §217] and broken the bond of the family—in the wider sense of the clan [see §181]—their

poverty leaves them more or less deprived of all the advantages of society, of the opportunity of acquiring skill or education of any kind, as well as of the administration of justice, the public health services, and often even of the consolation of religion, and so forth (§241).

This is a penetrating analysis of the dynamics of poverty in modern civil society. Hegel depicts perfectly the now-familiar spiral of poverty and its accompanying alienation from all the institutions of society. Particularly perceptive is his observation that the poor man still has the needs developed within civil society and shared by all of its members. Poverty has not dulled his need for social acceptance, 'the need of the particular to assert itself in some distinctive way' (§193).

'When civil society is in a state of unimpeded activity' (and it is the purpose of the public authority and the legal system to see to it that—so far as it is possible—it is in this, its rightful state), 'it is engaged in expanding internally in population and industry' (§243).[11] While the population is increasing, 'the amassing of wealth is intensified' by the generalisation of workers according to their needs and the increased sophistication of technology, 'because it is from this double process of generalisation that the largest profit is derived' (§243) (and, of course, the profit motive is the perfectly appropriate motive for civil society). At the same time, the division of labour 'results in the dependence and distress of the class [*Klasse*] tied to work of that sort, and these again entail inability to feel and enjoy the broader freedoms and especially the spiritual [*geistigen*] benefits of civil society' (§243).

Hegel goes on to describe how the disenchantment of alienated labour degenerates into extreme poverty: when the already low living standard of the working class declines below a certain level 'and when there is a consequent loss of the sense of right and wrong, of honesty and self-respect which make a man insist on maintaining himself by his own work and effort, the result is the creation of a rabble [*Pöbel*[12]] of paupers' (§244). How vividly Hegel describes the spiritual decay, the loss of human dignity which often accompanies poverty. 'A rabble is created only when there is joined to poverty a disposition of mind, an inner indignation against the rich, against the government' (§244A).

Poor people come to the point where they may refuse to work, as an act of defiance against the rich, because they know their impoverishment has created 'conditions which greatly facilitate the concentration of disproportionate wealth in a few hands' (§244). (This last observation, incidentally, is sufficient to convince me that Hegel had at least a tentative realisation of the law of political economy according to which 'the necessary consequence of competition is the accumulation of capital in a few hands'.[13]) The rabble refuses to work, but it demands 'to receive subsistence as a right' from the rich; because it knows that the poverty which prompted its downfall is 'a wrong done to one class [*Klasse*] by another' (§244A).

'It hence becomes apparent,' Hegel concludes, 'that despite an excess of wealth civil society is not rich enough, i.e. its own resources are insufficient to check excessive poverty and the creation of a penurious rabble' (§245). He notes that 'poverty in itself does not make men into a rabble' (§244A); but dealing with the problem of the rabble will demand discovery of 'the general causes of penury and general means of its relief' (§242). And so Hegel attempts to solve 'one of the most disturbing problems which agitate modern society' (§244A), the problem of poverty.

He considers several possible solutions. First, direct grants or alms could be given to the poor from 'the endowments of rich hospitals, monasteries, and other foundations' (§245) or out of the beneficence of 'the wealthier classes [*Klassen*]' (§245). This private almsgiving is in itself, however, an admission of the failure of the public authority, since 'public social conditions . . . are to be regarded as all the more perfect the less (in comparison with what is arranged publicly) is left for an individual to do by himself as his private inclination directs' (§242R).

As an alternative to this private charity, Hegel suggests that the public authority (*Polizei*) take the place of the family, to provide food and shelter and to try to rid the poor of the 'laziness of disposition, malignity, and the other vices which arise out of their plight and their sense of wrong' (§241). This suggestion, however, places the public authority in a dilemma : subjective freedom, manifest as the right to private property, must be preserved at all costs; this right to property 'has attained its recognised actuality as the protection of property through the administration of justice' (§208). One of the functions of the public authority is to guarantee that the decisions of the court of justice be obeyed : i.e. that the right of private property be safeguarded; that 'undisturbed safety of person and property be attained' (§230). But Hegel himself admits (§243) that the economic system based on the preservation of subjective freedom leads inexorably to the 'dependence and distress of the class tied to work of that sort' (§243)—that is, the class of wage-labourers. Hegel is suggesting (§241) that the public authority help the poor, while it is the economic system which the public authority (especially its coercive branch) is committed to protecting that is responsible for generating that poverty in the first place.

Hegel acknowledges this tension himself when he says that 'freedom of trade should not be such as to jeopardise the general good' (§236A). Hegel is certainly not a laissez-faire liberal. He is worried, however, by the consideration that with either one of the suggested remedies—private donations or welfare-statism—'the needy would receive subsistence directly, not by means of their work, and this would violate the principle of civil society and the feeling of individual independence and self-respect in its individual members' (§245).[14]

In a conflict between alleviating hunger and preserving the 'self-respect' of the hungry individual, Hegel seems to choose the latter. In fact, he seems to speak approvingly of the situation in Scotland, where it was decided that the most direct measure against poverty, loss of dignity, laziness and so on was 'to leave the poor to their fate and instruct them to beg in the streets' (§245R); presumably, such displays of individual initiative were good for their sense of 'shame and self-respect—the subjective bases of society' (§245R).

Hegel wants to avoid direct aid, from whatever source, so he considers an alternative solution : 'the opportunity to work' or, in contemporary parlance, 'work incentive programmes'. This would increase production, however—and the whole problem was created in the first place by an excess of production : 'the evil consists precisely in an excess of production and in the lack of a proportionate number of consumers who are themselves also producers' (§245). When the technology in an industry develops to the point that that industry produces more commodities than it can sell, it has to lay off a number of its workers. These laid-off workers are thereby deprived of the wages which enable *them* to buy the commodities produced by that industry; as a result, demand decreases further and more workers are laid off. Hegel's point—one commonly made by the political economists whom he had read—was that work which boosted production without radically increasing spend-ing-power and demand for those products would only serve to aggravate the problem.

Almost out of desperation, then, having admitted that 'civil society is not rich enough, i.e. its own resources are insufficient to check excessive poverty and the creation of a penurious rabble' (§245), Hegel suggests one final possible solution : colonisation. The 'inner dialectic of civil society' drives a specific civil society 'to push beyond its own limits and seek markets, in other lands which are either deficient in the products it has overproduced, or else generally backward in industry, etc.' (§246). The mature civil society is driven to colonise by an increase in population. In colonising, 'it supplies to a part of its population a return to life on the family basis in a new land' (§248). So, colonisation, by siphoning off excess labour and providing new markets for the products of the work incentive programmes, may be a temporary solution to the problem of poverty. Hegel has indeed given us an excellent account of the reasons for the historical phenomenon of colonisation[15]; but by its very geogra-phical limitations—sooner or later, every market in the world will be saturated with the surplus products of the mature civil society—we must conclude that colonisation is an inadequate solution to the problem of poverty in the metropolis.

Hegel makes no secret of the fact that he conceives the public authority primarily as an agency for controlling the anarchic economic forces within civil society. Because the commodity-pro-ducing economy is a system of interdependence, the activities of one person are likely to affect other members of civil society : 'this universal aspect makes private actions a matter of contingency which escapes the agents' control and which either does or may injure others and wrong them' (§232). In other words, within civil society, private actions (actions to do with property, the economy) have public consequences; the need for a public authority, there-fore, is indicated, to supervise and regulate private transactions.

The common good is foremost in Hegel's mind in this discussion. When it comes to a clash of interests between a producer and his customers, Hegel points out that this is not simply a transaction between one individual and another; rather is it between a producer and 'the public'. And Hegel will not allow the public interest to be jeopardised by the behaviour of a particular producer: 'The right to the exercise of control in a single case (e.g. in the fixing of the prices of the commonest necessaries of life) depends on the fact that, by being publicly exposed for sale, goods in absolutely universal daily demand [staple foodstuffs, basic clothing, etc.] are offered not so much to an individual as such but rather to a universal purchaser, the public' (§236). The public authority has to provide for such *public* necessities as 'street-lighting, bridge-building, the pricing of daily necessaries, and the care of public health' (§236A).

Hegel considers two alternative ways of looking at the problem of economic inequalities. On the one hand is the interventionist or 'welfare state' viewpoint. On the other is the Smithian laissez-faire viewpoint, which holds that the public authority has no business interfering in the free interplay of economic forces: if left to its own devices, the market will automatically provide for the needs of everyone. Hegel tries to accommodate the two, but comes down in favour of endeavouring to guarantee the common good: 'The individual must have a right to work for his bread as he pleases, but the public also has a right to insist that essential tasks shall be properly done. Both points of view must be satisfied, and freedom of trade should not be such as to jeopardise the general good' (§236A).

The status of the public authority and the state are, thus, very similar: both are expressions of communality or universality in human life. The difference is that membership of the state is not something optional; it is the highest embodiment of human rationality in the modern world. 'Since the state is spirit objectified, it is only as one of its members that the individual himself has objectivity, genuine individuality and an ethical life' (§258R). In the state, 'unification pure and simple is the true content and aim of the individual, and the individual's destiny is the living of a universal life' (§258R). This emphasis on universality is, of course, quite appropriate in the state.

Civil society, on the other hand, is the sphere of particularity: 'its specific end is . . . the security and protection of property and personal freedom' (§258R). Strong central control—such as that exercised by the public authority—should not be necessary in civil society. Such curbing of individual freedom is out of place in civil society, which is, after all, founded on individual freedom: '[Particular] interest invokes freedom of trade and commerce against control from above' (§236R). But Hegel realises that unfettered self-interest will lead to social ills and ultimately to anarchy : 'the more blindly [private interest] sinks into self-seeking aims, the more it requires such control to bring it back to the universal. Control is also necessary to diminish the danger of upheavals arising from clashing interests' (§236R).

The public authority, then, attempts to keep civil society from destroying itself, by regulating economic relations and searching for palliatives for the widespread poverty that is an inevitable out-growth of an exchange economy. But the activity of the public authority is perceived by the members of civil society as interference in their private affairs : 'its control takes the form of an external system and organisation for the protection and security of particular ends and interests *en masse*' (§249). And this is precisely the antagonistic relation between the free individual and the govern-ment which Hegel is most concerned to harmonise in the *Philosophy of Right*. The debilitating conflict between the individual and an alien government must be overcome. The free individual must identify with the power of the state as his own power, so that control by the state will be perceived as self-regulation by the free citizens of a rational state.

In the *Realphilosophie*, Hegel expressed this challenge to the integrating power of political institutions in terms of the dual character of modern Man (terms handed down by Rousseau), Man as a member of civil society and Man as a citizen of the state : 'Both individualities are the same. The same (individual) provides for himself and his family, works, enters into agreements etc.; and at the same time also works for the universal and has it as an end. From the former viewpoint he is called *bourgeois*, from the latter *citoyen*' (*JR* II, 249). The two most important mediating links between the egoism of civil society and personal identification with the common weal in the state are the social classes or estates [*Stände*] and the corporations or trade guilds [*Korporationen*]. The isolated, free individual can be integrated into the harmonious social totality by becoming a member of a class or of a corporation.

The Universal Within Civil Society: the Korporationen

It would probably be helpful to emphasise at the outset that Hegel's *Korporation* has nothing at all to do with what we refer to today as corporations : industrial/financial conglomerates such as ITT,

IBM and General Motors. Nor is Hegel referring to what we call trade unions, since trade unions represent (in theory, at least) the interests of *wage-labourers* in opposition to the employers in a given industry. Hegel sees the *Korporation* as representing the interests of a particular industry in general. The *Korporation* (I shall use the German form of the word henceforth to emphasise Hegel's special use of it) is much more like the trade guild of feudal times: Hegel himself intimates this when he argues against the trend towards 'the abolition of *Korporationen* in recent times' (§255A).[16]

Korporationen are particularly important for mediating the isolation of members of the business class (*Stand des Gewerbes*), since this class 'is essentially concentrated on the particular' (§250). In a *Korporation,* individuals sharing some common economic or professional bond (members of the various professions, artisans or tradesmen, businessmen) come together to form an organisation which will represent their common interest. This is an important step in integrating the many competing economic interests of the individuals in civil society : 'The implicit likeness of such particulars to one another becomes really existent in an association, as something common to its members' (§251). Although the members come together primarily to further their own individual interest (a quite appropriate motive in civil society), 'a selfish purpose, directed towards its particular self-interest, apprehends and evinces itself at the same time as universal' (§251). Although the *Korporation* consists of a number of people primarily interested in their own selfish economic ends, however, it is also an important agent of cooperation and *social* integration : 'its purpose is . . . to bring an isolated trade into the social order and elevate it to a sphere in which it gains strength and respect' (§255A). And the individual members of the *Korporation* share in that new-found strength and respect. The *Korporation* also has a more specifically political role : it represents the interests of its members in the legislature. The *Korporationen,* therefore, collectively articulate and represent the interests of civil society vis-à-vis the state : this serves to elevate the members of civil society to a higher ethical level, by involving them in 'work of a public character over and above their private business' (§255A).

It is clear from what he says in these passages that Hegel is describing a system of economic association which was fast disappearing, even in his own day. The Hegelian *Korporation* corresponds to an era when tradesmen and artisans (and bankers) were self-employed. Before the advent of factory mass-production, a shoemaker, for example, was self-employed; he was his own boss. Hegel seems to see the *Korporation* as an association which represents the interests of all these *independent* shoemakers. Now admittedly, we still have some medieval-style professional bodies, such as the British and American Medical Associations and the Incorporated Law Society, which manage to represent the interests of their members quite effectively, by retaining strict control over their own particular profession and by vigorous and effective lobbying of government. The craft and trade guilds, however, have become obsolete (and had almost become obsolete in Hegel's day), with the development of industry. The era of the individual journeyman has given way to a system of dependent factory-labour. It is obvious throughout this section that Hegel is including the former shoemaker who now owns a shoe factory in his *Korporation;* but that he does not include the labourer (whether formerly a master shoemaker or not) who now works for a wage in the shoe factory.

A *Korporation* has the right 'to protect its members against particular contingencies' (§252) and 'to provide the education requisite to fit others to become members. In short, its right is to come on the scene like a second family for its members' (§252). This is a giant step on the road towards the true solidarity of the state. 'Within the *Korporation* the help which poverty receives loses its accidental character and the humiliation wrongfully associated with it' (§253R). Lest this deceive us, it must be pointed out that Hegel is referring to poverty *within* the *Korporation* : should an estate agent, or perhaps a tailor, fall upon hard times, he would be helped out by his fellow estate agents or the guild of master tailors, as the case may be. This kind of mutual insurance against hardship promotes fraternity and is a bulwark against individual insecurity : 'Unless he is a member of an authorised *Korporation*, . . . [an individual's] livelihood and satisfaction become insecure. . . . The wealthy perform their duties to their fellow associates and thus riches cease to inspire either pride or envy, pride in their owners, envy in others' (§253R).

It is quite clear from the foregoing that Hegel considers the *Korporation* to be an extremely important mediating institution : in fact, 'the sanctity of marriage and the dignity of *Korporation* membership are the two fixed points round which the unorganised atoms of civil society revolve' (§255R). Yet he makes it equally clear that there is no place in the *Korporation* for the people who work in the factories; much less for the 'penurious rabble' of paupers. 'The *Korporation* member is to be distinguished from a day labourer or from a man who is prepared to undertake casual employment on a single occasion' (§252R).

This specifically excludes the entire class of people dependent for their survival on the economic uncertainties of factory labour; and the *Pöbel*, none of whom would be in a position to provide the necessary proof of 'regular income and subsistence' (§253). They would not be admitted to a *Korporation* and are, as a result, excluded from the organisational framework of Hegel's state. Hegel —more as an afterthought—does remark later that 'it is of the utmost importance that the masses should be organised, because only so do they become mighty and powerful. Otherwise, they are nothing but a heap, an aggregate of atomic units' (§290A). But in Hegel's civil society and state, the labouring masses *are* nothing but a heap of atomic units, since they may not become members of a *Korporation*. They are thereby excluded from citizenship in the state, since 'unless he is a member of an authorised *Korporation* . . . an individual is without rank or dignity, his isolation reduces his business to mere self-seeking' (§253R).

The State: the Harmony of the Private and the Public

Having described the *Korporation*—and, indeed, all of civil society —Hegel makes the transition to the state proper. In the state, the individual person is raised to universality through his identification with the various political institutions of mediation : the monarchy, the bureaucracy, the Assembly of Estates. In this process, individual concrete freedom is finally recognised explicitly as being necessary for the development of self-consciousness in history : 'The principle of modern states has prodigious strength and depth because it allows the principle of subjectivity to progress to its culmination in the extreme of self-subsistent personal particularity, and yet at the same time brings it back to the substantive unity and so maintains this unity in the principle of subjectivity itself' (§260).

In the modern state, 'duty and right are related in one and the same relation' (§261R). In doing something for the common good,

I realise that I am thereby confirming my own freedom as a fully participating member of a rational community. In the modern state, claims Hegel, individual freedom and communal responsibility, right and duty, the private man and the public man are finally united in a higher synthesis. This higher synthesis in the state does not detract in any way from the individual freedom proper to civil society, since civil society is subsumed in the state; freedom receives its full significance—which would never have been recognised within the one-sided confines of civil society—when raised to the context of the state.

In Hegel's dialectical terminology, the subjective freedom of civil society is *aufgehoben* or 'sublated' in the state, which is the *unity* of subject and object, of the private person and the citizen. Hegel explains elsewhere just what has happened in the historical transition from civil society to the state : 'What is sublated is not thereby reduced to Nothing. . . "To sublate" [*aufheben*] has a two-fold meaning in the language : on the one hand it means to preserve, to maintain, and equally it also means to cause to cease, to put an end to. . . . Thus what is sublated is at the same time preserved; it has only lost its immediacy but is not on that account annihilated.'[17] Civil society has been transcended in the state; but its essential features have also been preserved. As well as describing the transition in history from civil society to the modern state, this is also how Hegel sees the relation between civil society and the state in the modern world.

It is precisely because of the fact that civil society is preserved in its entirety within the framework of Hegel's state that I have dwelt so long on his description of the many conflicts and antagonisms within civil society—the sphere of the private individual, the economic 'war of everyone against everyone else'. Hegel has indeed suggested ways in which the severe human problems endemic to civil society can, hopefully, be mitigated (through the regulatory actions of the public authority, primarily). But he refuses to challenge the most fundamental principle of civil society : the free individual's pursuit of his own selfish ends. And this fundamental principle has been recognised and institutionalised in the modern world as a series of individual rights. Furthermore, civil society has its own institutions (e.g. the public authority and the *Korporationen*) designed to safeguard those rights. The question now is : how is Hegel going to describe a unified and harmonious political structure which contains within it all those individualistic forces which seriously threaten to tear it apart?

The political structure which he describes as the rational modern state depends for its overall unity on the following institutions: (*a*) a hereditary monarchy, in which the position of the monarch as symbol of the unity of the state cannot be challenged by factions within civil society, thanks to his hereditary accession to the throne; (*b*) a politically neutral state bureaucracy, relieved of the necessity of having to satisfy physical needs and thereby immune to the particularistic pressures of civil society; and (*c*) an Assembly of Estates, in which representatives of the monarchy, the bureaucracy and the social classes (*Stände*) of civil society meet to determine exactly how the interests of all the individuals in civil society can be harmonised in the state.

It is not important for us to examine in detail exactly *how* Hegel sees each of these institutions contributing to the overall unity of the state. Suffice it to say, at this stage, that Hegel was confident that he had successfully described the rational, harmonious state. It is, however, clear that the free individuals of civil society who are not members of the 'universal class' are expected to participate in the state through the medium of their *Stände*.

The *Stände* ('social classes' in civil society, 'Estates' in the political arena of the state) are the crucial link between the two spheres of human life: the private and the public. Civil society is the sphere in which mutual antagonism and social division is most apparent. In the remainder of this book, therefore, I shall ignore the monarchy and the bureaucracy and confine my analysis, for the most part, to the Assembly of Estates.

6

The Working Class and the Rational State

Hegel's 'Criterion of Rationality'

The success or failure of the Assembly of Estates as a medium of social integration will determine whether or not Hegel, in the *Philosophy of Right*, succeeded in the ambitious enterprise on which he had embarked : to describe the rational, harmonious state. 'This book,' he says calmly in the Preface, 'is to be nothing other than the endeavour to apprehend and portray the state as something inherently rational.'[1] In order to decide whether Hegel has succeeded in describing the rational modern state, I shall first try to identify what I shall call Hegel's personal 'criterion of rationality'.

To help us grasp what exactly Hegel was personally committed to in a 'rational' state, I would like to refer back to the first three chapters, in which I attempted to elicit Hegel's motivation for writing a system of philosophy : a system which includes a philosophical treatment of social and political experience. I concluded then that Hegel's philosophy was a response to his deeply-felt experience of dissonance and fragmentation throughout the world around him : in particular, the conflict between the individual and the community, between private ends and the public good. His system was conceived as an attempt to harmonise the many apparently conflicting aspects of human experience in a comprehensive description of reality. This philosophical description would demonstrate the inherent rationality of the world and of history by highlighting the interconnectedness of the dissonant elements in it.

At first, Hegel, confronted with the disintegration of modern Germany, seemed to hanker after the solidarity of the Greek *polis*. But he realised that that had been an unconscious kind of solidarity. The individual did indeed participate fully, in cooperation with his fellow-citizens, in affairs of the state; but he never stopped to question the idea of the identity of private and public goals. The citizen of the *polis* took this identity of interests for granted; he had no idea of his own power to decide otherwise. Such *instinctive* solidarity was no longer possible, since the appearance of self-conscious freedom in the history of European Man. This individual freedom was one of the hallmarks of modern society; and to return to the unconscious, merely 'felt' harmony of the *polis* would be to deny modern Man his right to individual freedom, an essential aspect of his personality.

So, Hegel was aware of the dual nature of modern Man: on the one hand, there is the *universal* aspect of human nature, which acknowledges the interdependence of all the people in a community; on the other hand, the *particular* aspect, which merely uses the community agencies and other people as instruments for the further-ance of its own selfish ends. And Hegel recognised that these two aspects of human nature—although they may, at first sight, appear somewhat contradictory—are inextricably linked together in our lives. On the one hand, a political community in which no indi-vidual initiative was tolerated would clearly be unthinkable. On the other hand, there is the typical individual who declares angrily : 'The state never did anything for me, except take my hard-earned money in taxes and send me off to fight in wars; I'll look after myself !' But even the most extreme individualist could be brought to see that those very rights, which he is so anxious to protect from governmental interference, are meaningful only in a social setting.

We can think of this dichotomy as a conflict—within each one of us—between the private individual who looks after his own interests first and foremost, regards other individuals primarily as competitors, and resents any governmental regulation of economic matters as an unwarranted infringement on his rights; and the citizen who demonstrates his loyalty and commitment to the com-munity by participating freely in public affairs for the furtherance of the common good. We can also refer to this dichotomy, in the terms used by Hegel in the *Philosophy of Right*, as the conflict between (subjective) particularity and (objective) universality.

'The right of the subject's particularity,' says Hegel in the *Philo-sophy of Right*, 'his right to be satisfied, or in other words the right of subjective freedom, is the pivot and centre of the difference between antiquity and modern times. This right in its infinity is given expression in Christianity and it has become the universal effective principle of a new form of civilisation' (§124R): civil society, which is 'the achievement of the modern world' (§182A). 'In civil society each member is his own end, everything else is nothing to him' (§182A). Subjective freedom cannot be denied; it is the 'fate' of modern man. We have seen, however, in the previous chapter, how subjective freedom threatens at all times to get out of control, since 'in civil society, universal and particular have fallen apart' (§184A). But this must not be allowed to happen, since 'the truth is the whole', as Hegel says in the famous dictum.[2] Applied to the realm of human relations, this means that the ethical ideal for a free individual consists of living entirely in and for the people (*Volk*) to which he belongs (*SPR* 419).

In civil society, however, we find that particularity, or subjective freedom, threatens to destroy the social order of the community. It is imperative, therefore, that 'while granting the right [of subjectivity], the whole order must at the same time retain strength enough to put particularity in harmony with the unity of ethical life' (§185A). Put in more concrete terms, a way must be found of integrating all the competing elements of civil society—the realm of particularity—into the structure of the state. And this is precisely what Hegel sets out to do in the *Philosophy of Right*. We can now say, then, that Hegel's 'criterion of rationality', in his social and political philosophy, is harmony between the particular and universal aspects of human nature. The rational state, for Hegel, is the political structure within which the diverse and disparate elements of particularity in civil society are integrated into a harmonious community.

Now, at no time does Hegel claim to be describing a Utopia in the *Philosophy of Right* : just as the course of history sometimes runs up blind alleys, so we must allow room for some degree of irrationality in Hegel's 'rational state'. We must also remember, however, that Hegel's main concern in writing the *Philosophy of Right* is to describe the institutions by means of which the mutually antagonistic factions of civil society are integrated into the state and come to identify with the authority of the state : 'What is of the utmost importance is . . . that my particular end should become identified with the universal end, or otherwise the state is left in the air. The state is actual only when its members have a feeling of their own selfhood and it is stable only when public and private ends are identical' (§265A).

Given Hegel's claim, therefore, that the 'rational state' is the political organism in which particularity and universality are harmonised, in which the particularity of civil society is integrated into the universality of the state, it is quite in order, I think, to ask Hegel : how is the class of people who labour for wages integrated into the rational state? If we find that this class—the majority in civil society, upon whom the whole society depends for the production of its wealth—is *not*, in fact, integrated into the state, this gives us cause for some serious reservations concerning Hegel's success in his stated enterprise.

Wage-Labourers and the Korporation

There are two ways, according to Hegel, in which an isolated individual in civil society initiates the process of his integration into the community : he becomes a member of a *Korporation*; and he takes his place as a member of a social class (*Stand*). I examined the section on the *Korporation* briefly in the last chapter; I would now like to have another look at what Hegel says about it and emphasise the fact that he seems to exclude the working *Klasse* from its ranks.

Hegel deems it absolutely crucial that there be some organisation in civil society which the atomistic member of the business class can join. This organisation is the *Korporation,* a middle term between absolute atomism and the universality of the state : 'Under modern political conditions, the citizens have only a restricted share in the public business of the state, yet it is essential to provide men —ethical entities—with work of a public character over and above their private business' (§255A). Even though the individual joins the *Korporation* for a primarily selfish reason, the very fact that he has to cooperate with other people—even on a limited scale— serves to mitigate his own social isolation. If we can imagine a continuum from pure particularity to pure universality, membership of a *Korporation* is one of the first steps away from particularity and towards universality : 'Unless he is a member of an authorised *Korporation* . . . an individual is without rank or dignity, his isolation reduces his business to mere self-seeking, and his livelihood and satisfaction become insecure' (§253R). If he is not a member of a *Korporation* the individual is completely alienated from the community; members of a *Korporation* serve 'to bring an isolated trade into the social order and elevate it to a sphere in which it gains strength and respect' (§255A).

Hegel mentions various qualifications for membership of a *Korporation*. The most important one stipulates that 'the *Korporation* member [*Gewerbsmann*] is to be distinguished from a day labourer [*Tagelöhner*] or from a man who is prepared to undertake casual employment on a single occasion. The former . . . is, or will become, the master' (§252R).[3] This stipulation excludes two groups of people from membership in a *Korporation*. The first group is the *Pöbel*, the rabble of chronically unemployed paupers, who have suffered loss of 'the sense of right and wrong, of honesty and the self-respect which makes a man insist on maintaining himself by his own work and effort' (§244). This class—by virtue of its continuing inability to secure employment—can have no access to Hegel's agencies of mediation and they are, as a result, doomed to total and perpetual alienation from the state.

Secondly, the large class of those who sell their labour for wages is also excluded from membership in the *Korporation*. Hegel specifically excludes from membership the day labourer (*Tagelöhner*) —the man who sells his labour from day to day. It is, surely, hard to believe that Hegel—especially after the horrifying descriptions of factory labour that he wrote in his Jena manuscripts—could possibly have been thinking of wage-labourers as 'masters' or even potential 'masters'. It is true that Hegel does not repeat any of his Jena descriptions of alienated labour in the *Philosophy of Right*; he does, however, refer to 'the dependence [*Abhängigkeit*] and distress [*Not*] of the class tied to work of that sort', i.e. factory labour (§243). Hegel acknowledges that workers are at the mercy of the uncertainties of the factory system : the spectre of unemployment perpetually hangs over them, because of the 'subdivision and restriction of particular jobs' (the division of labour) and the rapid development of new industrial technology.

The *Korporation*-member must have a skill and a reasonable expectation of a 'regular income and subsistence' (§253). Does this not render the wage-labourer ineligible for membership? I think so, since wage-labourers (except for the very few, if any, who in Hegel's day had some kind of a contract) are constantly at the mercy of the market and may be dismissed at any time. These are hardly likely candidates for membership in Hegel's *Korporation*.

If Hegel were to claim, even so, that he did mean to include factory-workers and other wage-labourers in his *Korporation*, I would have to express my surprise that members of the class 'tied' to dehumanising wage-labour—and thereby deprived of the ability 'to feel and enjoy the broader freedoms and especially the spiritual [*geistigen*] benefits of civil society' (§243)—should be considered as candidates for membership of an organisation which admitted only 'masters'. In any case, I find it very difficult to define *Gewerbsmann* (businessman) so as to include a wage-labourer. I must conclude, therefore, that all the members of the *Klasse* of industrial and agricultural wage-labourers are excluded from membership of a *Korporation*, one of Hegel's most important agencies of mediation between the particularity of civil society and the universality of the state.

Wage-labourers and Social Class

The second—and more crucial—medium of integration between the particular and the universal, in Hegel's state, is his system of class-divisions. The social classes into which civil society is divided are originally a function of the emerging division of labour :

> The infinitely complex, criss-cross, movements of reciprocal production and exchange, and the equally infinite multiplicity of means therein employed, become crystallised, owing to the universality inherent in their content, and distinguished into general groups. As a result, the entire complex is built up into particular systems of needs, means, and types of work relative to these needs, modes of satisfaction and of theoretical and practical education, i.e. into systems, to one or other of which individuals are assigned—in other words, into class-divisions (§201).

There are three classes in civil society : the immediate or agricultural class; the reflecting or business class; and the universal class or the bureaucracy.

Much more important than its function of merely defining the occupation of the individuals, however, is the integrating function of the social class. The process of integration occurs in two stages : in the first stage, the isolated individual is integrated into the framework of civil society; then, the system of classes or estates furnishes the most significant link between civil society and the state, by providing the individual with a channel of input into the deliberations of the legislature. This is how the individual comes to see the laws of the state as his laws, and not laws promulgated by an alien power. Only through membership of a class, therefore, can particularity and universality be reconciled in the free citizen of a state.

In the first instance, membership of a social class rescues the completely isolated individual in civil society from the oblivion of extreme particularity : one can imagine the unattached individual, disoriented, with no means of identification, neither for his own benefit nor for others : 'A man actualises himself only in becoming something definite, i.e. something specifically particularised; this means restricting himself exclusively to one of the particular spheres of need' (§207). This is how a person first obtains recognition by others and respect for himself : 'When we say that a man must be a "somebody", we mean that he should belong to some specific social class. . . . A man with no class [*Stand*] is a mere private person and his universality is not actualised' (§207A). The classless (*standlos*) individual will never achieve integration into the framework of the rational state. In the second phase of integration, the Assembly of Estates—the elected representatives of the social classes—represent the interests of civil society in the affairs of the state. Hegel complained that political theories which insist on keeping civil society and political life apart 'involve the idea that the classes [*Stände*] of civil society and the Estates [*Stände*] which are the "classes" given a political significance, stand wide apart from each other. But the German language, by calling them both *Stände,* has still maintained the unity which in any case they actually possessed in former times' (§303R).

The estates are the most important medium of integration between the particularity of civil society and the universality of the state :

> The specific function which the concept assigns to the Estates is to be sought in the fact that in them the subjective moment in universal freedom—the private judgement and private will of the sphere called 'civil society' in this book—comes into existence integrally related to the state. . . . Regarded as a mediating organ, the Estates stand between the government in general on the one hand and the nation broken up into particulars (people and associations) on the other (§301R, §302).

As a member of a *Stand,* then, one is a social—and fully human—being. A person who is not a member of a *Stand,* however, will not be integrated into the social structure of the state; to him, the government will always be an alien institution. Bearing this in mind, I shall now examine Hegel's system of classes (*Stände*), in the *Philosophy of Right*, to see what provision he makes—if any—for the rabble of paupers and for the *Klasse* of wage-labourers.

The second of Hegel's three social classes is the business class (*Stand des Gewerbes*). He divides this class into three sub-classes: craftsmanship (*Handwerksstand*), manufacture (*Fabrikantenstand*) and trade (*Handelsstand*). The craftsmen 'work to satisfy single needs in a comparatively concrete way and to supply single orders' (§204); and the merchants and financiers deal with 'the universal medium of exchange, money, which actualises the abstract value of all commodities' (§204). Neither of these classes has any difficulty in being integrated into *Stände* and into corporations. It is the manufacturing branch of the business class, however, that poses a problem.

This is the only class which Hegel does not denote exclusively by the more traditional term *Stand*. Throughout his work, in referring to the two sub-classes within the manufacturing branch of the business *Stand*, Hegel uses the term *Klasse*. In fact, as early as his Jena 'System der Sittlichkeit', Hegel refers to the group of people who depend on wage-labour for a livelihood and who actually produce the wealth of the society as '*die arbeitende Klasse*' (*SPR* 498)—literally, the working class. He retains this usage in the *Philosophy of Right* when he refers to 'the dependence and distress of the class [*Klasse*] tied to work of that sort' (§243). He also widens the usage to refer to the luxury and extravagance of the 'business classes [*Klassen*]' (§253R); and when he remarks that the burden of maintaining the poverty-stricken masses 'might be directly laid on the wealthier classes [*Klassen*]' (§245).

Now, perhaps one should resist the temptation—in a post-Marxian world—of reading too much into Hegel's references to the conflicting groups within the *Stand des Gewerbes*—the '*arbeitende Klasse*' and the '*gewerbtreibenden Klassen*'. But, even if we translate *Klasse* with an innocent, unloaded term such as 'group', it seems to me to be undeniable that Hegel had an intuitive grasp—in an embryonic and unsystematic form, at least—of an institutionalised conflict within the manufacturing sub-*Stand* between the people who actually labour in the factories and those who own the factories and employ the labourers: groups that later came to be known as 'proletariat' and 'bourgeoisie'.[4]

This detail of intellectual history is not really important for the purposes of my argument, however. The really important point is that Hegel departs from his overall schema of *horizontal* divisions in society (*Stände*) to draw our attention to the *vertical* division between the *Klassen* within the manufacturing *Stand*—the *Stand* which is, after all, the motive force of civil society and the modern state.[5] That 'vertical' conflict is, surely, what he is referring to when he says that 'once society is established, poverty immediately takes the form of a wrong done to one class [*Klasse*] by another' (§244A).

I would now like to glance at what Hegel says about factory-labour. In fact, he says very little about it in the *Philosophy of Right*. This in itself is very surprising, given his passionate descriptions of work in factories, mines, etc., in his Jena manuscripts. Although Hegel's tone is now more muted, he does refer (almost in passing), in the *Philosophy of Right*, to the same aspects of the labour process which he had been so concerned about in the earlier writings. One of the main themes in the Jena works was the total dependence of the individual worker on an economic system which is 'an alien power, over which he has no control' (*SPR* 492). This notion of the relationship of 'need and necessity' (*JR* II, 233) between the worker and his work reappears in two passages in the *Philosophy of Right*, when Hegel speaks of those individuals who are 'tied [*gebundenen*]' (§236, §243) to industrial wage-labour. It is true, nonetheless, that Hegel's language is now much more sober and restrained.

Perhaps it was because he was now writing a book for publication; but nowhere in the *Philosophy of Right* does he use language as rousing as this : 'Masses of the population are condemned to labour in the factories, manufacturing works, mines, etc.; work which is totally stupefying, unhealthy, insecure and faculty-stunting' (*JR* II, 232). While the rhetoric is missing, however, the substance of what Hegel was saying does reappear in the *Philosophy of Right*. New developments in mechanisation and the technology of mass-production result in 'the dependence and distress of the class [*Klasse*] tied to work of that sort, and these again entail inability to feel and enjoy the broader freedoms and especially the spiritual [*geistigen*] benefits of civil society' (§243).

Hegel does not elaborate at all on what he means by the inability to enjoy the 'broader freedoms' and 'the spiritual benefits' of civil society. I take him to be referring to the kinds of spiritual and ethical benefits accruing to membership in a *Stand* and in a *Korporation*. For one thing, Hegel points out several times that the factory worker has no security of tenure : on the one hand, industries 'are dependent on conditions abroad and on combinations of distant circumstances' (§236); on the other hand, 'when civil society is in a state of unimpeded activity . . . the amassing of wealth is intensified by generalising (a) the linkage of men by their needs, and (b) the methods of preparing and distributing the means to satisfy those needs' (§243). These developments, together with the problem of overproduction (§245), conspire to make the life of the factory worker extremely insecure.

Unfortunately, Hegel does not spell this out in the *Philosophy of Right*. But I take him to be making the same point, in the last-quoted passage, which he made so dramatically in the *Realphilo-sophie* : 'Branches of industry which supported an entire class of people suddenly collapse because of [changes in] fashion or because of a drop in prices due to discoveries in other countries, etc.; and this whole mass of people are abandoned to helpless poverty' (*JR* II, 232). Hegel repeats in the *Philosophy of Right* this point that the security of the factory worker is subject to the caprice of the market mechanism. The factory worker is living from day to day : he can be—and is—periodically dismissed to what Marx was later to call 'the relative surplus-population or industrial reserve army.'[6] And this is why he is excluded from membership of a *Korporation*, which is open only to a *Gewerbsmann*, who is 'master' and secure in his employment (§252R).

If the problem afflicting the *Klasse* of wage-labourers is the alienated and dehumanising character of their labour, which in turn deprives them of the broader freedoms and spiritual benefits of civil society, the situation of the *Pöbel* is somewhat different : the rabble of paupers is alienated from the social structure, not because of the alienated character of its labour, but because of the fact that it has no labour at all. Nor does the *Pöbel* pose a problem in civil society just because of its poverty. As Hegel points out : 'poverty in itself does not make men into a rabble; a rabble is created only when there is joined to poverty a disposition of mind, an inner indignation against the rich, against society, against the government, etc.' (§244A). Their disposition of mind, their sense of being wronged, is a more important factor in their exclusion from the benefits of society than their extreme poverty.

Quite clearly, there is no place in the system of *Stände* for the rabble, such is the extent of their anger and alienation. Hegel merely suggests, in a half-hearted way, a few palliatives to mitigate their extreme distress and to attempt to reintegrate them back into civil society. But the problem proves essentially insoluble within the terms of civil society, so he gives up and dismisses them to their fate : i.e. the 'Scottish solution' or no solution at all. Some might be inclined to accuse Hegel of callousness towards these victims of commodity-producing society. In abandoning the rabble to their 'fate' and instructing them to beg in the streets, he does sound, uncharacteristically, like the government official who proclaimed in unemployment-plagued Detroit that 'the right to suffer is one of the joys of a free economy'.[7] This would, however, be unfair to Hegel, who was very conscious of the fact that alternative solutions to the problem of feeding the rabble either involved an excess of production or some kind of a handout. And Hegel would do almost anything to avoid advocating direct subsistence payments, since 'this would violate the principle of civil society and the feeling of individual independence and self-respect in its individual members' (§245).

If we accept Hegel's concern for the self-respect of the rabble, however, we must wonder whether he feels so strongly about the lack of self-respect prevalent among the factory workers and other wage-labourers. Admittedly, the workers do have a job, which the rabble do not. The 'disposition of mind', however, the anger and hostility, must be very similar in both cases. Hegel says, in connection with the rabble, that 'the feeling of individual independence and self-respect' was 'the principle of civil society' (§245). But factory labour produces 'the dependence and distress of the class tied to work of that sort, and these again entail inability to feel and enjoy the broader freedoms and especially the spiritual benefits of civil society' (§243). In this way, factory workers in civil society are deprived of their human or civil rights (see §209R); and of spiritual benefits such as the right of insight into right and wrong (see §132).

'Mere Private Persons'

We must now decide whether or not the working *Klasse* qualifies for inclusion in a *Stand*; and the only likely candidate is the manufacturing class (*Fabrikantenstand*). Hegel gives us no indication one way or the other. He probably wishes us to take it for granted that the class of wage-labourers is a part of the manufacturing class, since this would further his efforts at integrating all the elements of civil society into the state. But he really gives us no reason to believe that the workers would wish to have any form of social liaison with their employers. On the contrary, his description of the dynamics of modern industry is largely concerned with the clashes between the workers and the factory-owners. In fact, 'once society is established, poverty immediately takes the form of a wrong done by one class [*Klasse*] to another' (§244A). Almost everything Hegel says about the class of wage-labourers suggests that they have much to be bitter about. So, perhaps we can apply the criterion that was applied to the rabble : what was judged was not their poverty, but their 'disposition of mind'. Thus when I claim that Hegel has failed to integrate the working class into his system of classes, I say so *not* because they are poor (and really, this case is quite distinct from the case of the rabble), but because of the 'disposition of mind' induced by their experience of dehumanising and insecure factory labour.

What, then, are some of the implications of Hegel's failure to accommodate wage-labourers in a *Stand*? The first—and major—implication is the political one. If the worker is not integrated into the social system, he is thereby denied a voice (through the Estates) in the legislature and excluded from the joys of citizenship in the state. As the young Marx expressed it : 'The class in need of immediate labour, of concrete labour, forms less a class of civil society than the basis upon which the spheres of civil society rest and move'.[8]

Apart from the fact that the Assembly of Estates, and through it the government, is closed to the isolated worker, there are other important implications for the worker who is not integrated into a *Stand*. For example, since the members of the working *Klasse* remain 'mere private persons', whose worth cannot be recognised by others in the society, then civil society as Hegel describes it is incapable of guaranteeing to the large majority of its members the kinds of rights which he demands of his own rational state. The example of one such right will suffice.

It is axiomatic that Hegel is, throughout his social and political writings, more concerned about the ethical wellbeing of the members of the society than he is about their physical welfare. Now, the rational state is, according to Hegel, a social organism in which the actualisation of certain 'rights' is guaranteed. Among these rights is 'the right of insight into the good':

> The right of the subjective will is that whatever it is to recognise as valid shall be seen by it as good, and that an action . . . shall be imputed to it as right or wrong, good or evil, legal or illegal, in accordance with its *knowledge* of the worth which the action has in its objectivity. . . . The right of giving recognition only to what my insight sees as rational is the highest right of the subject (§132, §132R).

Now, how is the subject to acquire this knowledge of what is right and wrong? He will acquire it, says Hegel, in an 'ethical order' (*sittlichen Wirklichkeit*): 'The right of individuals to be subjectively destined to freedom is fulfilled when they belong to an actual ethical order. . . . When a father inquired about the best method of educating his son in ethical conduct, a Pythagorean replied: "Make him a citizen of a state with good laws"' (§153, §153R). In this, Hegel is going right back to his own youthful dictum that 'the only ethical totality is a people [*ein Volk*]'. 'In an *ethical* community [*sittlichen Gemeinwesen*], it is easy to say what man must do, what are the duties he has to fulfil in order to be virtuous: he has simply to follow the well-known and explicit rules of his own situation. Honesty [*Rechtschaffenheit*] is the general character which may be demanded of him by laws or custom' (§150R).

Hegel is saying here that individuals have a right to belong to an actual ethical order with which they can identify: a 'station in life' with readily-identifiable rights and duties, in which they can achieve self-respect. Also, a degree of ethical formation enabling them to carry out the duties of their station as self-conscious rational subjects and not simply performing a blind habit or responding to coercion. In civil society, says Hegel, this right is guaranteed when the individual becomes a member of a *Stand*: 'a man actualises himself only in becoming something particularised, i.e. something definite; this means restricting himself exclusively to one of the particular spheres of need. In this class-system the ethical frame of mind therefore is honesty and *esprit de corps*' (§207).

It seems to me, however, that the member of the working *Klasse*, in Hegel's civil society, is not integrated into a social class: he cannot, therefore, 'actualise himself' in an ethical community. Since he is deprived of the ethical formation which is normal in such a community—in which one learns 'the duties of the station to which he belongs'—it appears that the *standlos* wage-labourer is thereby denied 'the highest right of the subject . . . [the] right of insight into the good' (§132R). Hegel felt that society owed its members a vision of 'the good' and a reasonable opportunity of attaining it. The vision is gained as a member of a *Stand* (an ethical community), in which the individual learns to see 'the good'; and also learns to see the appropriate restrictions and duties as good. This is an important incidence of the harmony of the universal and the particular. Since the wage-labourer is not a member of the *Stand,* however, the vision of the good remains for him unattainable. And this is but one of a number of important rights denied to the labourer who is not integrated into Hegel's system of social classes.

I have endeavoured to show that Hegel's attempt to describe the rational state as the harmony of the universal and particular was effectively sabotaged by his failure to integrate the rabble of paupers and working class into his system of social classes and Estates. It is hardly likely, however, that Hegel would have agreed with my appraisal; and it is interesting to speculate briefly on how he might respond to my conclusion.

From his own words in the *Philosophy of Right,* I think that he would probably agree that he has a problem with the rabble of paupers: 'Despite an excess of wealth civil society is not rich enough, i.e. its own resources are insufficient to check excessive poverty and the creation of a penurious rabble. . . . The important question of how poverty is to be abolished is one of the most disturbing problems which agitate modern society' (§245, §244A).

Hegel seems to be of the opinion, however, that the existence of a 'rabble'—even a rabble continually growing in numbers—is peripheral to civil society. Although it is an inevitable outgrowth of market forces, it does not threaten to undermine fundamentally the fabric of civil society. He would probably argue that although the rabble is indeed a wound in civil society, it is not a fatal one. While only a relatively small number of people is involved, the existence of a permanent rabble is little more than an irritant. And, of course, it shows how any attempt to describe a fully rational organism or structure is doomed to failure. By virtue of human imperfection, Hegel would claim, one can always expect a little accidentality in the midst or on the fringe of a rational totality.

Hegel would probably defend himself vehemently concerning the position of the working class; and claim that the *Klasse* of factory-workers does indeed form part of the manufacturing sub-class. It is very difficult to know what to reply. On the one hand, one might be tempted to allow that Hegel must *know,* since he wrote the book, after all, and must have thought about the problem of absorbing the working class into the *Stände.* But he was also purporting to *describe* the modern state; and he had given descriptions previously which had painted a very different picture.

So I would not be prepared to let the matter rest there. I would confront Hegel with what he wrote in 1801–6 about the plight of the working class : 'Work becomes more and more dead absolutely, it becomes mechanical work. The skill of the individual worker becomes all the more limited, to an infinite degree, and the consciousness of the factory worker is degraded to the ultimate state of dullness' (*JR* I, 239); and much more, highlighting the alienation of the factory-worker. I would be very curious to know why Hegel dropped almost all references to alienated labour in the *Philosophy of Right.* Surely factory conditions had not improved so much in the intervening fifteen years. On the contrary! Does he now feel that workers have reconciled themselves to 'work that is totally stupefying, unhealthy, insecure and faculty-stunting' (*JR* II, 232), to the extent that they wish to throw in their lot with the captains of industry, in the *Fabrikantenstand*?

Perhaps Hegel would simply claim—as he does in the 'Preface' to the *Philosophy of Right*—that he is merely describing the modern state as it is; there are many things wrong with it, but it's the best there is. It is therefore inherently rational and we must resign ourselves to it, no matter how unpalatable that might be. I would have to point out that it seems to me, from reading his early works, that he has considerable personal investment in the quest for harmony between universal and particular in the modern world. Is it possible that he was too horrified by the degree of conflict in the modern world to face up to it? Much easier, more reassuring to forget about vertical class divisions and revert to the old system of horizontal classes or estates; to issue a call for solidarity among the members of the manufacturing class.

Finally, I would ask Hegel to consider that the two major

E

problems afflicting the modern state—widespread poverty and dehumanising, alienated labour—are both directly attributable, as he himself admitted, to an economic system which is based on the sanctity of private property. Hegel would probably reply that private property is the embodiment of subjective particularity, the freedom of modern Man; its abolition would be unthinkable.

Hegel and Contemporary Capitalist States

Should Hegel insist on claiming that he has indeed integrated the working *Klasse* into the business *Stand*, there is another way of approaching this issue, which might convey more clearly my reservations: we can compare the modern state as Hegel describes it in the *Philosophy of Right*, with actual examples of existing modern states. Having applied an 'internal' test of the coherence of Hegel's description of the modern state, we can now apply an 'external' test of its coherence. I have argued above that Hegel has failed to convince me that he has successfully integrated the working *Klasse* into the social order, through their membership of a *Stand*. Although he does not specifically exclude them from membership of a *Stand*, he does specifically exclude them from membership of a *Korporation*, which is the first stage in the social integration of individuals. Furthermore, it seems strange that Hegel should expect us to believe—after the descriptions he himself has given us of the conflicts *within* the manufacturing class of civil society, between those who work for a wage and those who own the productive property—that the working *Klasse* could just be integrated into the manufacturing class (the *Fabrikantenstand*) quite naturally; or, indeed, that they really have a place in any of the *Stände* in civil society.

Whether he would wish to admit it or not, therefore, Hegel describes a social order in which the vast majority of the population do *not* identify with the state-power: the working *Klasse*, since they are not integrated into the social system, perceive the authority of the state as an alien power. As Hegel himself points out, this inevitably leads to clashes of interest in civil society (§236, §236R), in which the public authority has to intervene. And because of the dynamics of this conflict, the public authority does not behave and is not perceived by the working *Klasse* or a neutral regulatory agency.

The working *Klasse*—if we follow the logic of Hegel's description of civil society—is 'alienated' from the state. This point is borne out if we examine existing modern states. When we examine these states empirically, and the relations between groups within them, we find that the hoped-for harmony between private interests and the general public good has not, in fact, materialised. Marx demonstrated this in considerable detail with regard to the state of his day.

A Hegelian might protest that a genuine rational state—as Hegel conceived it—has just not been fully developed yet; but that this empirical fact does not in any way detract from Hegel's theoretical achievement in describing the rational modern state in the *Philosophy of Right*. He might quote Hegel to the effect that 'in considering the Idea of the state, we must not have our eyes on particular states' (§258A). Or he might claim that these so-called states to which I am referring are merely examples of 'the external state, the state based on need, the State as the Understanding envisages it' (§183).

Now, I would agree entirely with Hegel's defender that the typical modern states with which we are familiar today do indeed fail lamentably to embody Hegel's ideal of harmony between private interests and the public good. But if we look at some of the salient social and political features of these advanced capitalist countries, we can see that they correspond almost exactly with the institutions considered by Hegel to be the essential features of the rational modern state.

What exactly constituted a rational modern state, according to Hegel (always remembering, of course, that Hegel was purporting to describe the rational state, not devise one)? The details of his description can be reduced to a few all-important institutions; institutions which, he felt, successfully mediated between the fundamental selfishness of the individual and the universal power of the state. First, the public authority was seen by Hegel as 'a middle term between an individual and the universal possibility, afforded by society, of attaining individual ends' (§236A). Every advanced capitalist state has a Hegelian public authority in the shape of governmental regulatory agencies, which see it as their role to ensure the smooth operation of the free enterprise economy: in the United States, for example, two of the better-known regulatory agencies are the Federal Trade Commission (established 1914) and the Securities and Exchange Commission (1913); in Britain, there is, for example, the Monopolies and Mergers Commission (1948). These public regulatory agencies—and many others like them—are essential features of modern capitalist states.

In his analysis of the state proper, Hegel describes three institutions which are the most crucial agencies of mediation between private and public interests in the state: the constitutional monarchy; the 'universal class' or the state bureaucracy; and the representative Assembly of Estates. Now, every modern state has some form of career civil service, devoted exclusively to the business of administering the affairs of the state. Most civil services or state bureaucracies actually correspond quite closely to Hegel's model. Secondly, every advanced capitalist state has some form of representative assembly. The actual method of representation in the different countries is irrelevant. The important factor unifying all National Assemblies is that they all—including Hegel's—aim to represent the interests of all the elements of society in the deliberations of the Assembly on national affairs.

Finally, many modern capitalist states (e.g. Great Britain, Sweden, the Netherlands) have a hereditary constitutional monarch as their head of state. All others have a president (or a head of state with a similarly imposing title) with a varying degree of executive power. Again, I think the variations are unimportant. The head of state is a symbol of the *unity* of the state—the Many represented in the One. It is this concept—that the President, no matter who he or she might be, represents *all* the people of the United States—that is expressed in the fairly common conviction that 'you can say what you like about the President, but you must never show disrespect for "the office of the Presidency" '.

I can now make my point succinctly (and deal with Hegel's defender at the same time). In his description of the modern state, Hegel names four institutions which, he claims, will ensure a harmonious and creative relationship between the individual members of civil society and the state. These four institutions are fully operative (with insignificant variations) in all modern capitalist states. But these institutions do not, typically, ensure a harmonious and creative relationship between the individual members of civil society and the state. On the contrary! Our own everyday experience tells us that the institutions of state do *not* look after all our interests equally, as disinterested agencies of mediation between the private and the public spheres. As a result, therefore, government and the whole apparatus of state, in modern capitalist societies, is generally seen by those who have not the political power that money and property can buy, as an alien force : the government is not something into which I have any significant input, over which I have any significant control or influence. In sum, it is not 'my government'. From our comparison between the theory of the *Philosophy of Right* and the reality of modern capitalist states, therefore, we can conclude that the social order of the modern state—and especially the relationship between civil society and the state—is *not* as Hegel describes it in the *Philosophy of Right*.

Conclusion

What are we to make, then, of Hegel's unsuccessful attempt to describe the rational modern state? Perhaps, most of all, we are impressed by his penetrating and far-sighted analysis of the capitalist, commodity-producing economy and of its corresponding political institutions. We can also admire his honesty : he described the dynamics of civil society as he observed it—tearing itself apart— even though he could not come up with a satisfactory solution to the problem. We must be thankful, too, that he did not resort to the traditional liberal wishful-thinking according to which the unregulated capitalist economy would right itself and guarantee the freedom and prosperity of all the citizens.

How, then, do we explain the attempt to heal class antagonisms with an integrated system of estates which excludes the working class? To account for this, I think we must return to my thesis concerning the motivation for Hegel's philosophical endeavours. He desperately wanted to give a philosophical account of man and his world, which would synthesise all the antagonisms and conflicts in experience into a higher, coherent totality. Instead, he himself must have been deeply impressed—and depressed—by the near-anarchic conditions of modern society. He was obviously very disturbed by the sordid scar on the face of the modern world, 'the unrighted wrong' caused by the capitalist economy. With that, however, he stressed the integration and solidarity in the state brought about by the *Stände* even more vehemently, perhaps even with a sigh of relief.

To demonstrate that Hegel *in fact* indulged in a mystification of reality in his efforts to articulate a philosophical grasp of human experience—which I have endeavoured to do—is one thing; to suggest that this was done consciously and with a desire to deceive, is something else, for which I know of no evidence. It is a curious fact, nonetheless, that appeals to national solidarity in the face of impending class conflict have rung out with monotonous frequency in recent history.

Perhaps philosophy *qua* philosophy can only interpret and understand the world, not change it. But this does not automatically compel us (as Hegel would have us do) 'to recognise reason as the rose in the cross of the present and thereby . . . enjoy the present.'[9] 'When philosophy paints its grey in grey,' wrote Hegel, 'then has a form of life grown old.'[10] When Hegel painted his grey in grey in the *Philosophy of Right*, the resulting treatise was a disturbing picture of the evils wrought by the capitalist economic system and the reverence for private property. Hegel always strenuously refused to peer into the crystal ball; but was he suggesting that that particular form of life 'had grown old'? And if so, was it not to be followed by a new 'form of life'?

Although he refused to dissociate the concept of subjective freedom from the sanctity of private property, Hegel's ideal of a synthesis of personal freedom and solidarity remains. But then, this Hegelian ideal is precisely what socialism is all about. 'The owl of Minerva [philosophy] spreads its wings only with the falling of dusk,' declared Hegel. In a short time, however, arrives a new dawn.

Notes

CHAPTER 1 (1–19)

1. On the *Goethezeit*, see W. H. Bruford, *Germany in the Eighteenth Century*, second ed., Cambridge 1965.

2. Knut Borchardt, 'The Industrial Revolution in Germany 1700–1914', in *The Fontana Economic History of Europe: The Emergence of Industrial Societies, Part One*, edited by Carlo M. Cipolla, Glasgow 1973, 86.

3. Especially *An Essay on the History of Civil Society*, Edinburgh 1767, translated into German in 1768.

4. Millar's *The Origin of the Distinction of Ranks*, London 1771, was translated into German in 1772 and was reviewed by Herder in *Frankfurter Gelehrte Anzeige* in the same year.

5. Ferguson, 182–3.

6. *Ibid.*, 183.

7. See J. G. Herder, *Auch eine Philosophie der Geschichte zur Bildung der Menschheit* (1774), Frankfurt am Main 1967, 60–61.

8. *Voltaire's Correspondence*, edited by Theodore Besterman, LX, Geneva 1961, 64. Voltaire habitually referred to Rousseau's work as 'son contrat insocial': see, for example, *Voltaire's Correspondence*, XLIX, 46; LXI, 92; LXIII, 85.

9. *Hegels Theologische Jugendschriften (Early Theological Writings)*, edited by H. Nohl, Tübingen 1907, 3–29. This fragment is not translated in the Knox volume. It is translated in H. S. Harris, *Hegel's Development*, 481–507. The translation here is my own.

10. It was the editor Nohl who first used the term 'theological' in connection with Hegel's writings of the period 1790–1800.

11. 'Hegel's early anti-theological phase', *Philosophical Review* LXIII (1954), 3–18.

12. *The Young Hegel: studies in the relations between dialectics and economics*, trans. R. Livingstone, London 1975, 8–16.
13. See X. Leon, *Fichte et son temps*, I, Paris 1922, 173. See also A Cobban, *A History of Modern France*, third ed., Harmondsworth, 1963, I 177–8 : 'All over France political clubs were formed by local revolutionaries. Establishing a system of correspondence with the Paris Jacobins, many of them came to adopt its name and look to it for leadership. By 1793 there were probably between five and eight thousand such clubs.'
14. See W. Dilthey, *Die Jugendgeschichte Hegels*, Berlin 1905, 13–14.
15. See J. Ritter, *Hegel und die französische Revolution*, Cologne 1957, 18.
16. See Paul Chamley, 'Les origines de la pensée économique de Hegel', *Hegel-Studien* III (1965), 226.
17. *Confidential Letters upon the previous constitutional relation of Wadtland (Pays de Vaud) to the City of Bern: a full unmasking of the former oligarchy of the Bernese Estate. Translated from the French of a deceased Swiss* [an exiled lawyer from Vaud] *with additional comments*, Frankfurt-on-Main 1798. For a short account of the *Confidential Letters*, see Z. A. Pelczynski's introductory essay to *Hegel's Political Writings*, translated by T. M. Knox, Oxford 1964, 9–12.
18. See Gisela Schüler, 'Zur Chronologie von Hegels Jugendschriften', *Hegel-Studien* II (1963), 111–59, for the detailed dating of Hegel's early fragments, which is vital for an understanding of his development.

CHAPTER 2 (20–37)

1. See *Philosophy of Right*, §183, where Hegel defines civil society as 'the external state, the state based on need, the state as the understanding envisages it [*Not- und Verstandesstaat*]'.
2. I take the liberty of using the slightly anachronistic term 'alienation' to refer to the splits in modern life, because of the close similarity of Schiller's terminology ('*fremd*' and '*Fremdling*') to the term later used by Hegel (in the *Phenomenology* and subsequently) and by Marx to denote 'alienation', viz. '*Entfremdung*'. Already, in Tübingen, Hegel had referred to men under the influence of private religion as '*menschliche Empfindungen fremd*' ('strangers to human feelings'). See *HTJ* 27.

3. Cf. Sir Eric Ashby (then vice-chancellor of The Queen's University of Belfast), in an address to the Congress of European Vice-Chancellors (Dijon, September 1959) : 'Science and invention have contributed to the destruction of European civilisation; but in science and invention lies one hope for its repair' (*Le Figaro,* 10 Sept. 1959). Quoted by Wilkinson and Willoughby in Schiller, 236.

4. *Basic Documents on Human Rights,* ed. I. Brownlie, London 1971, 8.

5. Jean Hyppolite, *Studies on Marx and Hegel,* London 1969, 58.

6. See Cobban, *op. cit.,* 238.

7. *An Inquiry into the Principles of Political Oeconomy, Being an Essay on the Science of the Domestic Policy in Free Nations in which are particularly considered Population, Agriculture, Trade, Industry, Money, Coin, Interest, Circulation, Banks, Exchange, Public Credit and Taxes,* London 1767, new edition in 2 vols, ed. A. Skinner, London : Edinburgh 1966.

8. See P. Chamley, *Économie politique et philosophie chez Steuart et Hegel,* Paris 1963, 136–8, 210–12; also P. Chamley, 'Les origines de la pensée économique de Hegel', *Hegel-Studien* III (1965), 235–43. This section owes much to the meticulous research of Professor Chamley, the results of which are presented in the above-mentioned works.

9. See Schüler, 'Chronologie', 146.

10. Chamley, 'Les origines de la pensée économique', 239.

11. See Schüler, 'Chronologie', 146.

12. Steuart, *Inquiry,* ed. Skinner, I, 34–6.

13. See Schüler, 'Chronologie', 146.

14. Steuart, *Inquiry,* I, 28.

15. *Ibid.,* 16.

16. *Ibid.,* 56.

CHAPTER 3 (38–55)

1. Quoted by Rudolf Haym in his summary of the remainder of the pamphlet (now lost), in *Hegel und seine Zeit,* Berlin 1857, 66.

2. F. Hölderlin, *Hyperion or The Hermit in Greece,* trans. W. R. Trask, London 1965, 164.

3. J. Bryce, *The Holy Roman Empire,* second ed., London 1912,

400–401n. For a description of Germany at this time, see also Borchardt, *op. cit.*, 76–90.
4. *The German Ideology*, ed. C. J. Arthur, London 1970, 98.
5. See Schüler, *op. cit.*, 133.

CHAPTER 4 (56–72)

1. The term *Sitten* can also mean 'manners' (cf. *moeurs* in French). Since having good manners, however, usually consists of doing 'the done thing' or what is customary and expected of one, this usage also ties in with Hegel's technical meaning of *Sittlichkeit*.
2. We have already discussed Hegel's debt to Ferguson and Steuart; Chamley supports Hoffmeister's contention that Hegel first read Smith when he arrived in Jena (see 'Les origines', 253). Hegel uses Smith's example of the pin-factory workers in his *Realphilosophie I*, 239. He also refers to him specifically, on occasion: see, for example, *PR* §189R, in which he also mentions Say and Ricardo.

CHAPTER 5 (73–96)

1. For a helpful summary of the logico-metaphysical framework within which Hegel's discussion of civil society takes place (together with some enlightenment concerning Hegel's 'dialectical' terminology), see section 4 of Knox's foreword, *Philosophy of Right*, vii–x. Numbers in the text henceforth will refer to paragraphs in the *Philosophy of Right*, unless otherwise stated; numbers followed by R and A will refer to remarks and additions to the paragraphs respectively.
2. Hegel had made the distinction between the understanding (*Verstand*) and reason (*Vernunft*) in his very first essay, 'The Difference between the Systems of Philosophy of Fichte and Schelling' (see pp. 50–51).
3. See Vance Packard, *The Hidden Persuaders*, Harmondsworth 1960, 106–15, on 'Selling Symbols to Upward Strivers'.
4. Cf. Packard, *Hidden Persuaders*, 37: 'Among the subsurface motivating factors found in the emotional profile of most of us, for example, were the drive to conformity, need for oral stimulation, yearning for security. Once these points of vulnerability were isolated, the psychological hooks were fashioned and baited and placed deep in the merchandising sea for unwary

prospective customers.' See also Packard, 132–9, on the related 'psycho-seduction of children'; and 143–4, on 'psychological obsolescence'.

5. The term *Vermögen* which Hegel uses here (and which I translate as 'resources') has two meanings, one abstract and the other tangible. It can be used to refer to one's 'capacity' to do something, as when one says that 'it is not within my power' to do something; it can also designate one's 'assets' or total worth.

6. See Basil Bernstein, 'Social structure, language, and learning', *Education Research* III (1961), 163–76; see also the twenty-five articles in *Schooling and Capitalism*, ed. R. Dale, et al., London : Henley 1976, especially P. Henderson, 'Class structure and the concept of intelligence', 142–51; also Brian Simon, *Intelligence, Psychology and Education: a Marxist critique*, new ed. London 1976. For a useful survey of recent discussion on these and related topics, see Brian Simon, 'Contemporary Problems in Educational Theory', *Marxism Today* 20 (June 1976), 169–77.

7. Many would, of course, question this view. But people are certainly given an unequal start in life by virtue of the circumstances of their birth—and the deleterious effects can be the same.

8. Cf. the title of a work by William Grieg, a Scottish surveyor and civil engineer who worked in Ireland in the early nineteenth century : *Strictures on Road Police, containing the views of the present system, by which Roads are Made and Repaired*, Dublin 1818. Adam Smith lectured in Glasgow in 1763 on 'Justice, Police, Revenue and Arms'. See also Brian Chapman, *Police State*, London : New York 1970, especially Ch. 1, 'The origins of the term'.

9. The term translated by Knox as 'education'—*Bildung*—has a much wider meaning than simply learning 'the three R's' : it refers to the overall process of intellectual and cultural formation.

10. See also, for the importance of the concept of *Bildung* in Hegel's work and intellectual background, G. A. Kelly, *Idealism, Politics and History: sources of Hegelian thought*, Cambridge 1969, 341–8; and R. Pascal, ' "Bildung" and the Division of Labour', in *German Studies presented to Walter Horace Bruford*, London 1962, 14–28.

11. Cf. Adam Smith's remark that 'poverty seems to be favourable to generation', *Wealth of Nations,* I, Oxford 1976, 96, cited by Marx in *Capital,* London 1954, I, 602, n.l.

12. See Knox's note 88, *Philosophy of Right,* 361 : 'no single word is available for a mass of *rebellious* paupers, recognising no law but their own, and it is this which Hegel means'.

13. Marx, *Early Writings,* Harmondsworth 1975, 322. See pp. 63, 69 above. Hegel would have derived such laws of political economy from his reading of Adam Smith and the other classical political economists. The centrality of the concept of capital in classical economic theory was quite explicit as early as the *Tableau Économique* (1758) of François Quesnay (1694–1774). A. R. J. Turgot (1727–81) referred to the accumulated surplus of income over expenditure as 'a capital' (*Reflections on the Formation and the Distribution of Wealth* (1766), in *Turgot on Progress, Sociology and Economics,* translated by R. L. Meek, Cambridge 1973, 150). Furthermore, Turgot pointed out that 'the possessor of *capitals*' employs workmen and awaits 'the profit sufficient to compensate him for what his money would have been worth to him if he had employed it in the acquisition of an estate' (*ibid.,* 152). The first use of the term 'capitalist' which I have come across is also in Turgot : the 'capitalist' is 'the possessor of a movable capital' (*ibid.,* 153–82 *passim*). There is no evidence that Hegel read Turgot, but he certainly did read Adam Smith, probably upon his arrival in Jena in 1801; and *The Wealth of Nations* is an analysis of a fairly sophisticated 'capitalist' economic system. Smith not only made the important distinction between 'fixed capital' and 'circulating capital', but dwelt at length on 'the accumulation of capital'. The fundamental role of capital in the modern economy—an economy in which the conjunction of capital and labour produces profit—was even more clearly expressed in Jean-Baptiste Say's *Treatise on Political Economy* (1803) and David Ricardo's *Principles of Political Economy and Taxation* (1817), both of which Hegel read (see *PR* §189R).

14. On the function of work in liberating people from dependence on Nature, see §196.

15. Cf. Marx and Engels, *Communist Manifesto* : the only solution for 'the epidemic of over-production' is an expanding market; consequently, 'the need for a constantly expanding market for

its products chases the bourgeoisie over the whole surface of the globe'. In Marx and Engels, *Basic Writings on Politics and Philosophy*, ed. Lewis S. Feuer, London : Glasgow 1969, 52, 54.

16. In 1776, during his tenure as Controller General of France, Turgot issued an edict to suppress the guilds, which had degenerated into exclusive, caste-like organisations obstructing the freedom of labour. They were abolished completely in France in 1789.

17. *Hegel's Science of Logic*, trans. A. V. Miller, London : New York 1969, 107.

CHAPTER 6 (97–116)

1. *Philosophy of Right*, 11.

2. *Phenomenology of Mind*, trans. J. B. Baillie, New York 1967, 81.

3. Hegel's term *'der Meister'* is translated by Knox as 'master of his craft'. But *'Meister'* is probably just a direct translation by Hegel of the term 'master' used by Adam Smith and others (see Ferguson's *Essay*, 183) to designate the employer (the owner of stock or capital) in an industrial or agricultural enterprise. Smith, for example, habitually refers to the relationship between 'the master' and 'the workmen'. See, for example, Smith's discussion of 'the wages of labour' and industrial disputes, in *The Wealth of Nations*, I, 82–5. This merely reinforces my point that Hegel is restricting membership of the *Korporation* to employers, while excluding from membership those who work for them.

4. I have already drawn attention to Smith's discussion of conflicts between 'the masters' and 'the workmen' (see note 3 above). In a section of his *Reflections* (1766) headed 'Subdivision of the industrial stipendiary class into capitalist entrepreneurs and ordinary workmen', Turgot drew the distinction thus : 'The whole class which is engaged in meeting the different needs of society with the vast variety of industrial products finds itself, so to speak, subdivided into two orders : that of the entrepreneurs, manufacturers, and masters who are all possessors of large capitals which they turn to account by setting to work, through the medium of their advances, the second order, which consists of ordinary artisans who possess no property but their

own hands, who advance nothing but their daily labour, and who receive no profit but their wages' (*Turgot*, 153). Whether or not Hegel read Turgot, it is clear that by 1821 the division of the manufacturing sub-*Stand* into capitalist entrepreneurs and wage-earning workmen was both a well-established historical reality and taken for granted in the relevant literature.

5. I owe this particular terminology (i.e. 'horizontal' and 'vertical' divisions in Hegelian society) to Allen Wood (private communication).

6. *Capital*, I, 604.

7. Eisenhower aide Governor Howard Pyle, *New York Times*, 24 May 1956, 20.

8. *Critique of Hegel's 'Philosophy of Right'*, trans. Annette Jolin and Joseph O'Malley, Cambridge 1970, 81. (Marx's *Critique* deals only with §§261–313 of the *PR*.)

9. *Philosophy of Right*, 12.

10. *Ibid.*, 13.

Bibliography

Note: The bibliography below is far from exhaustive: I have listed only those works which have a bearing on Hegel's social and political thought. I give priority to English translations of Hegel's works, citing works in the original German only when an English translation is unavailable. Finally, I list other works cited in the text and suggestions for further reading. The reader is referred to Walter Kaufmann's *Hegel: reinterpretation, texts, and commentary*, 469–86, for particularly valuable information concerning the several editions of Hegel's works. J. J. O'Malley et al. eds., *The Legacy of Hegel*, contains 'Hegel: a bibliography of books in English, arranged chronologically', by Frederick G. Weiss, 298–308. The list begins in 1971 and goes back to 1848.

WORKS BY HEGEL

English translations

'The Tübingen essay of 1793', translated by H. S. Harris, in his *Hegel's Development: Toward the Sunlight 1770–1801*, Oxford 1972, 481–507.

Early Theological Writings, translated by T. M. Knox, introduction by Richard Kroner, Chicago 1948.

Hegel's Political Writings, translated by T. M. Knox, with an introductory essay by Z. A. Pelczynski, Oxford 1964.

On the Difference between Fichte's and Schelling's System of Philosophy, translated and edited by Walter Cerf and H. S. Harris, Albany, N.Y. 1977.

Faith and Knowledge, translated and edited by Walter Cerf and H. S. Harris, Albany, N.Y. 1977.

Natural Law, translated by T. M. Knox, Philadelphia 1975.

Phenomenology of Mind, translated by J. B. Baillie, new introduction by George Lichtheim, New York 1967.

Hegel's Science of Logic, translated by A. V. Miller, London : New York 1969.
Philosophy of Right, translated by T. M. Knox, Oxford 1942.
Hegel's Philosophy of Mind, translated by William Wallace and A. V. Miller, Oxford 1971.

Untranslated works
Hegels Theologische Jugendschriften (Early Theological Writings), ed. H. Nohl, Tübingen 1907.
Briefe von und an Hegel (Hegel's Correspondence), ed. J. Hoffmeister, 4 vols, Hamburg 1952–60.
Dokumente zu Hegels Entwicklung (Documents on Hegel's Development), ed. J. Hoffmeister, Stuttgart 1936.
Erste Druckschriften (Early Publications), ed. G. Lasson, Leipzig 1928.
Schriften zur Politik und Rechtsphilosophie (Writings on Politics and the Philosophy of Right), ed. G. Lasson, Leipzig 1913.
Jenenser Realphilosophie I, ed. J. Hoffmeister, Leipzig 1932.
Jenenser Realphilosophie II, ed. J. Hoffmeister, Leipzig 1931.

OTHER WORKS

Asveld, Paul, *La pensée religieuse du jeune Hegel: liberté et aliénation*, Louvain : Paris 1953.
Avineri, Shlomo, *Hegel's Theory of the Modern State*, Cambridge 1972.
Bergmann, Frithjof H., 'The Purpose of Hegel's System', *Journal of the History of Philosophy* II (October 1964), 189–204.
Bernstein, Basil, 'Social structure, language, and learning', *Education Research* III (1961), 163–76.
Borchardt, Knut, 'The Industrial Revolution in Germany 1700–1914', in *The Fontana Economic History of Europe: The Emergence of Industrial Societies, Part One*, ed. Carlo M. Cipolla, London : Glasgow 1973.
Bourgeois, Bernard, *La pensée politique de Hegel*, Paris 1969.
Brownlie, Ian, ed., *Basic Documents on Human Rights*, Oxford 1971.
Bruford, Walter H., *Germany in the Eighteenth Century: the social background of the literary revival*, second ed., Cambridge 1965.
Bryce, James B., *The Holy Roman Empire*, second revised ed., London 1912.

Bülow, Friedrich, *Die Entwicklung der Hegelschen Sozialphilosophie*, Leipzig 1920.

Chamley, Paul, *Économie politique et philosophie chez Steuart et Hegel*, Paris 1963.

Chamley, Paul, 'Les origines de la pensée économique de Hegel', *Hegel-Studien* III (1965), 225–61.

Chapman, Brian, *Police State*, London : New York 1970.

Cobban, Alfred, *A History of Modern France*, third ed., 3 vols, Harmondsworth 1963.

Dale, R. et al. eds., *Schooling and Capitalism*, London : Henley 1976.

Dilthey, Wilhelm, *Die Jugendgeschichte Hegels*, Berlin 1905.

Ferguson, Adam, *An Essay on the History of Civil Society* (1767), new impression edited with an introduction by Duncan Forbes, Edinburgh 1966.

Fleischmann, Eugène, *La philosophie politique de Hegel*, Paris 1964.

Foster, Michael B., *The Political Philosophies of Plato and Hegel*, Oxford 1935.

Gray, J. Glenn, *Hegel and Greek Thought*, New York 1968.

Germino, Dante, 'Hegel as a Political Theorist', *Journal of Politics* XXXI (1969), 885–912.

Habermas, Jürgen, 'Labor and Interaction : Remarks on Hegel's Jena *Philosophy of Mind*', *Theory and Practice*, translated by John Viertel, London 1974.

Harris, H. S., *Hegel's Development: Toward the Sunlight 1770–1801*, Oxford 1972.

Haym, Rudolf, *Hegel und seine Zeit*, Berlin 1857.

Herder, Johann G., *Auch eine Philosophie der Geschichte zur Bildung der Menschheit* (1774), Frankfurt am Main 1967.

Hölderlin, Friedrich, *Hyperion or The Hermit in Greece*, translated by W. R. Trask, London 1965.

Hyppolite, Jean, *Studies on Marx and Hegel*, translated by J. O'Neill, London 1969.

Kaufmann, Walter, 'The Hegel myth and its method', *Philosophical Review* LX (1951), 459–86.

Kaufmann, Walter, *Hegel: reinterpretation, texts and commentary*, Garden City, N.Y. 1965.

Kaufmann, Walter, 'Hegel's Early Anti-Theological Phase', *Philosophical Review* LXIII (1954), 3–18.

Kaufmann, Walter, ed., *Hegel's Political Philosophy*, New York 1970.

Kelly, George A., *Idealism, Politics and History: Sources of Hegelian Thought*, Cambridge 1969.

Knox, T. M., 'Hegel and Prussianism', in *Philosophy* XV (January 1940), 51–63.

Kojève, Alexandre, *Introduction to the Reading of Hegel*, ed. Allan Bloom, translated by J. H. Nichols Jr., New York 1969.

Leon, Xavier, *Fichte et son temps*, 2 vols, Paris 1922–7.

Lukács, Georg, *The Young Hegel: Studies in the Relations between Dialectics and Economics*, translated by Rodney Livingstone, London 1975.

Marcuse, Herbert, *Reason and Revolution: Hegel and the rise of social theory*, new ed., London 1955.

Marx, Karl, *Capital: A Critique of Political Economy*, 3 vols, translated by Samuel Moore and Edward Aveling, London 1954.

Marx, Karl, *Critique of Hegel's 'Philosophy of Right'*, translated by Annette Jolin and Joseph O'Malley ed. with an introduction by Joseph O'Malley, Cambridge 1970.

Marx, Karl, *Early Writings*, introduced by Lucio Colletti, translated by Rodney Livingstone and Gregor Benton, Harmondsworth 1975.

Marx, Karl, *The German Ideology*, ed. C. J. Arthur, London 1970.

Marx, Karl, and Friedrich Engels, *Basic Writings on Politics and Philosophy*, ed. Lewis S. Feuer, London : Glasgow 1969.

Millar, John, *The Origin of the Distinction of Ranks; or, an Inquiry into the Circumstances which Give Rise to Influence and Authority, in the Different Members of Society*, third ed., London 1781.

O'Malley, J. J. et al. eds., *The Legacy of Hegel: proceedings of the Marquette Hegel Symposium 1970*, The Hague 1973.

Packard, Vance, *The Hidden Persuaders*, Harmondsworth 1960.

Pascal, R., ' "Bildung" and the Division of Labour', in *German Studies presented to Walter Horace Bruford*, London 1962.

Pelczynski, Z. A. ed., *Hegel's Political Philosophy: problems and perspectives*, Cambridge 1971.

Plant, Raymond, *Hegel*, London 1973.

Reyburn, Hugh A., *The Ethical Theory of Hegel: a study of the philosophy of right*, Oxford 1921.

Riedel, Manfred, *Bürgerliche Gesellschaft und Staat bei Hegel*, Neuwied and Berlin 1970.

Riedel, Manfred, *Studien zu Hegels Rechtsphilosophie*, Frankfurt 1969.

Ritter, Joachim, *Hegel und die französische Revolution*, Cologne 1957.

Rosenkranz, Karl, *Georg Wilhelm Friedrich Hegels Leben*, Berlin 1844.

Rosenzweig, Franz, *Hegel und der Staat*, Berlin : Munich 1920.

Rousseau, Jean Jacques, *Émile*, translated by Barbara Foxley, London 1950.

Rousseau, Jean Jacques, *The Social Contract and Discourses*, translated with an introduction by G. D. H. Cole, revised ed., London 1973.

Schiller, J. C. Friedrich, *On the Aesthetic Education of Man, in a Series of Letters*, a bilingual edition edited and translated by Elizabeth M. Wilkinson and L. A. Willoughby, Oxford 1967.

Schüler, Gisela, 'Zur Chronologie von Hegels Jugendschriften', *Hegel-Studien* II (1963), 111–59.

Simon, Brian, 'Contemporary problems in educational theory', *Marxism Today* XX (June 1976), 169–77.

Simon, Brian, *Intelligence, Psychology and Education: a Marxist critique*, new ed., London 1976.

Smith, Adam, *An Inquiry into the Nature and Causes of the Wealth of Nations* (1776), general eds. R. H. Campbell and A. S. Skinner, textual ed. W. B. Todd, 2 vols, Oxford 1976.

Smith, Adam, *Lectures on Justice, Police, Revenue and Arms* (1763), ed. Edwin Cannan, Oxford 1896.

Steuart, Sir James, *An Inquiry into the Principles of Political Oeconomy* (1767), ed. Andrew S. Skinner, 2 vols, London : Edinburgh 1966.

Taylor, Charles, *Hegel*, Cambridge 1975.

Turgot on Progress, Sociology and Economics, translated, edited and with an introduction by Ronald L. Meek, Cambridge 1973.

Voltaire's Correspondence, ed. Theodore Besterman, 107 vols, Geneva 1953–65.

Weil, Eric, *Hegel et l'État*, Paris 1950.

Wiedmann, Franz, *Hegel: an illustrated biography*, translated by J. Neugroschel, New York 1968.

Index